DATE DUE

MR 17 '95			

DEMCO 38-296

BUYING SERIALS

A How-To-Do-It Manual
for Librarians

N. BERNARD BASCH
JUDY McQUEEN

HOW-TO-DO-IT MANUALS
FOR LIBRARIES
Number 10

Series Editor: Bill Katz

NEAL-SCHUMAN PUBLISHERS, INC.
New York, London   1990

Published by Neal-Schuman Publishers, Inc.
100 Varick Street
New York, NY 10013

Printed and bound in the United States of America

Library of Congress Cataloging-in-Publication Data

Basch, N. Bernard
    Buying serials : a how-to-do-it manual for librarians / N. Bernard
Basch, Judy McQueen.
        p. cm. — (How-to-do-it manuals for libraries : no. 10)
    Includes bibliographical references and index.
    ISBN 1-55570-058-6
    1. Acquisition of serial publications—Handbooks, manuals, etc.
2. Newspaper and periodical wholesalers—Handbooks, manuals, etc.
3. Booksellers and bookselling—Colportage, subscription trade
etc.—Handbooks, manuals, etc.   4. Newspaper and periodical
libraries—Handbooks, manuals, etc.   5. Libraries and booksellers—
Handbooks, manuals, etc.   I. McQueen, Judy.   II. Title.
III. Series.
Z692.S5B37   1990
025.2'832—dc20   90-49692
                                                    CIP

CONTENTS

PREFACE

Buying Serials had its origins in our belief that information is power. In our experience, the more library personnel know about serials publishing and serial vendors, the more responsible and effective their decisions on serials acquisitions. Similarly, those publishers and vendors who are most knowledgeable about library operations and priorities provide the most responsive services.

Information is power, but information on the tapestry of issues that influence serials acquisitions has not previously been readily available in one place. The purpose of *Buying Serials* is to provide readers with a basic appreciation of serial acquisition practices and possibilities.

Practices vary widely. There are no hard and fast rules. There is no single approach that can guarantee efficient and cost-effective acquisition of serial materials by libraries. The diversity of current practices is exceeded only by the range of possibilities for creative approaches to serials acquisitions. Some innovations arise because of the concerns of a single player in the serials supply chain—publisher, vendor, or librarian. Others develop through the pursuit of mutual interests by two or more parties. The more each party knows about the needs and concerns of the others, the more favorable the environment for the development of creative acquisitions opportunities of benefit to all.

While directed to the priorities and concerns of all practicing library personnel, students, and faculty members, *Buying Serials* is also intended to provide insight for serial publishers and vendors. Our objective is to maximize the value of serials acquisitions in the library community: to assist library staff in making serials available to users; to encourage vendors to offer service and pricing packages that meet the needs of libraries; and to alert publishers to the concerns of their library customers.

Judy McQueen
Buzzy Basch
Chicago
September 1990

INTRODUCTION

Serials are an essential library resource, providing an immediacy and depth of focus unrivalled by any other form of publication. They are expensive, however, and consume an increasing proportion of library materials funds. Prices are increasing more rapidly than inflation or materials budgets. The decision to purchase a serial entails an ongoing commitment of library resources: the recurring expenditure of funds to maintain the subscription and the continuing allocation of staff to monitor and process issue receipts. Responsible serials managers pursue all opportunities to maximize the return for monies spent on serials.

The serials acquisition process offers numerous opportunities for maximizing the return on serials investments: direct savings in the amount expended on the purchase of serials and indirect savings in labor and operations costs. Recognition of such savings requires an understanding of the policies and practices of serial publishers and an appreciation of the different methods of acquiring serials. Chapter One explores the role of serials in libraries, and publisher practices that affect serial acquisitions.

Libraries obtain serials by direct purchase from publishers, or by purchase through subscription agencies and vendors, by exchange with other institutions, and as gifts. Subscription agencies and vendors dominate serials acquisitions, processing at least half and, possibly, two-thirds, of the annual serials expenditures of U.S. libraries. Serials vendors utilize economies of scale, discounts from publishers, and sophisticated automated systems to provide subscription management services for libraries. Agencies generally give discounts to smaller public libraries and school libraries, and levy service or handling fees on most other accounts.

There is no magic formula that will determine the best method of serials acquisition for a library. Each library has different needs and priorities, and most libraries employ more than one approach to serials acquisition. What *is* essential is that each library establish its needs and critically evaluate its supply options. "Critical" is a key word. What works for most libraries will not necessarily work in the unique environment of an individual library. Thus, serials managers should identify and scrutinize *all* assumptions.

The issues that impact upon effective serials acquisitions decisions are not amenable to linear description. They mingle and intertwine. Approaches that may be most convenient for a library may be blocked by the policies and practices of serials publishers, by the guidelines of the library's administration, or by the constraints of the library's budget or staffing allocation.

In this book we examine the issues from the perspective of library use of serials subscription agencies. Most libraries obtain most of their serials from vendors. Gift and exchange are viable options for only a limited number of titles and institutions. A decision to order direct from publishers usually entails a conscious decision not to use a vendor. Such a decision must be as firmly based on an understanding of library needs and priorities and agency operations and services as a decision to use an agency. Chapter Two provides an overview of basic agency services, and Chapter Three explores the business aspects of agency operations.

A library seeking vendor service for serials acquisitions must clearly define its requirements and criteria for acceptable vendor performance. A successful library-vendor relationship requires that service expectations be realistic, based on an understanding of the range of agency service and pricing options and an appreciation of the supply factors that are outside the control of both libraries and vendors. The library must communicate its requirements to potential vendors, solicit service proposals, and choose a vendor or vendors. Selection will be facilitated if a library has clarified its objectives for seeking vendor support and determined its priorities for vendor selection. The formality of the vendor selection process will vary from library to library. In most situations a library will have the opportunity to clarify areas of concern with potential vendors and to negotiate a mutually acceptable service and pricing package with the vendors of preference. Chapter Four addresses needs definition, assessment of agency services, and vendor selection. The Appendix provides an overview of the range of automated services agencies offer libraries.

Professional responsibility and opportunities to maximize return on library expenditures do not end with vendor selection and initiation of service. This is only the beginning. The effective serials manager plays an active role in monitoring vendor performance, identifying and defining areas in which service falls below the agreed parameters, communicating any dissatisfaction, and working with vendors to resolve problems. These activities are the focus of Chapter Five.

1 SERIALS AND LIBRARIES

When most people think about libraries and library resources, they think about books. Depending on their experience, they may also think of newspapers, machine-readable data bases, video cassettes, magazines, and journals. Few make an unprompted distinction between materials produced as discrete and complete units—most books, sound recordings, and video cassettes—and those issued serially—newspapers, magazines, newsletters, periodicals, annual reports, yearbooks, abstracts, indexes, and the like. Yet, serials—publications issued at intervals and intended to continue indefinitely—are an essential resource for libraries, serving as the major vehicle for the distribution of current information.

Although serials are essential, they are also expensive. In some academic and research libraries, expenditures on serials account for more than 75 percent of the acquisitions budget. As per title price increases outstrip cost increases for other types of library material, and the number of serials published increases, serials are becoming more expensive. United States libraries currently spend more than $1 billion a year on serials. If the current rate of price and publication increase continues, the amount will increase to $2 billion by 1997.

Because of the ongoing nature of serials publications, a decision to subscribe to a serial usually commits acquisition funds for the year of purchase and for future years. Serials also require the continuing allocation of staff resources to handle the check-in, processing and claiming of the multiple pieces received against a single order. In addition to the costs of acquisition, other direct and continuing expenditures include storage and binding, cataloging, and catalog maintenance.

Library managers use a variety of techniques to maximize the return on expenditures for serials. In selection and acquisition, common practices include: periodic review of subscriptions to ensure that the titles in the collection match the needs of users and the mission of the library, and ongoing evaluation of such alternatives to direct acquisition as cooperative collection development, interlibrary resource sharing, document delivery services, and on-demand purchase of single articles or issues. Full use of local serials resources is facilitated by access techniques such as user-oriented cataloging and check-in procedures, and the use of abstracting, indexing and current contents tools such as remote online services or local CD-ROM files in hard-copy, and the machine-readable files of abstracts and contents data loaded on local automated library systems.

These procedures can have a significant impact on the value a library receives for its serials expenditures. However, the most direct returns occur in the effective management of the serials acquisitions process. This requires an awareness of the characteristics of serials and serial publishing, an understanding of the options for acquiring serials, and a considered analysis of the needs and priorities of the individual library situation.

WHAT IS A SERIAL?

Definitions abound, but it is difficult to find one that clearly distinguishes serials from other types of publications *and* encompasses all variants of the serials format. As a result, our efforts to define serials to board members, nonlibrary managers, or purchasing departments are often liberally sprinkled with qualifications and exceptions.

The second edition of the *Anglo-American Cataloguing Rules* defines a serial as:

> A publication in any medium issued in successive parts bearing numerical or chronological designations and intended to be continued indefinitely. Serials include periodicals; newspapers; annuals (reports, yearbooks, etc.); the journals, memoirs, proceedings, transactions, etc., of societies; and numbered monographic series. (page 622)

Most commentators include similar characteristics in their less formal definitions, producing variants such as that used by Taylor in *Managing the Serials Explosion*:

> A serial is a publication reproduced in more than one copy and more than one issue. It has a common name identifying the issues, and dating or numbering to show the distinction and connection between one issue and another. It has no intended point of completion.[1]

Or, a definition with special appeal for most serials librarians:

> . . . serials are those things that have the greatest probability of going awry, in the most parts, with the greatest frequency.[2]

United States librarians use "serial" as the inclusive term for works issued in parts and intended to continue indefinitely; British librarians use the term "periodical." To most North Americans, a periodical is a specific type of serial that is published regularly and includes articles by different authors—a journal. The British reserve the term "serial" for titles that are published annually, irregularly, or at intervals longer than a year.

Moreover, different libraries use different operating definitions, reflecting the types of serials critical to their service missions. In one library, the term "serials" may refer to the collection of annual reports essential to the parent corporation's business activities; in another the term refers to the periodic publications of a government statistical agency; and, in a third, to popular magazines and newspapers, the receipt or nonreceipt of which can be of great significance to individual patrons.

For our purposes serials may most usefully be defined as those publications which librarians and library suppliers treat as serials. Within this definition, serials can be divided into "periodical serials" and "non-periodical serials." Periodical serials are issued regularly, once a year or more frequently. Periodicals, newspapers, business and legal services are usually periodical serials. Non-periodical serials are issued less regularly and more infrequently: biennials, monographs in series, sets, multivolume series, and proceedings. Many commentators consider that annual publications straddle the two categories: annuals produced on a regular schedule—in May of each year, for instance—behave like periodical serials; annuals which routinely display irregular characteristics—the 1988 issue published in August 1988, the 1989 issue in March 1989, for example—have the characteristics of non-periodical serials.

SERIAL EXPENDITURES

Collectively, libraries spend enormous amounts of money on serials. For individual libraries, annual serial expenditures range from a few hundred dollars in small school and public libraries to more than $2 million in large academic research libraries. And the proportion of library materials budgets allocated to serials can be significant. In a survey of seventy-nine academic libraries conducted in 1985, three spent more than 75 percent of their materials budgets on serials; sixty-three spent 50 to 75 percent; only thirteen of the libraries allocated less than 50 percent of their acquisitions budgets to serials.[3]

The authors estimate that U.S. libraries spent more than $1 billion on serials in 1989:

Type of Library	Estimated Number of Libraries	Estimated Serial Expenditures
College and Academic	5,000	$390 million
Medical	1,700	$150 million
Public and School	16,000	$100 million
Government	2,000	$148 million
Law, Corporate and Other	5,000	$435 million
Totals	29,700	$1,223 million

Library expenditures on serials are increasing, driven by increases in the price of individual titles and acceleration in the number of titles published.[4] Attempts to cut the impact of serials costs on libraries have not stemmed the flow. Despite collection rationalization, resource sharing, and increasingly vocal objections to high price increases for materials from specific publishers, the trend continues. Although the rate of increase in serials expenditures may diminish, prices and expenditures will continue to escalate during the 1990s.

SERIAL PRICES

Throughout the 1980s serial price increases outstripped increases in both the consumer price index and the cost of monographs. One commentator summarized the frustration libraries experienced by drawing a parallel between the trend in serial prices and a Steve Martin joke:

> Martin recalls that in 1960 there were three Elvis Presley impersonators in the country; by 1980 there were 300 Elvis Presley impersonators; if present trends continue, he notes gravely, by 2020 one in every three Americans will be employed as an Elvis Presley impersonator![5]

Recent research has focused on the impact of price increases in academic libraries with an emphasis on the cost of titles from major commercial scientific, technical, and medical publishers. However, the issues affect all libraries. Due to the continuing nature of serials publications and collection development policies which favor multi-year runs of serials, price increases have a snowballing effect, impacting both current acquisition budgets and the allocation of funds in future years. In many libraries maintenance of the serials collection has severely eroded the funds available for the acquisition of monographs. Charles Hamaker has compared the economic impact of an academic library's investment in serials to the operation of an adjustable rate mortgage:

> Serial subscriptions are like a bad adjustable rate mortgage: they require a large down payment in the form of the purchase of backruns; they are dependent on yearly payments that seem to increase arbitrarily; they are without benefit of a cap or lid; and, continuing the mortgage analogy, when it is time to dispose of the purchase or stop making contributions to it, the negotiations with faculty and the flow of paper from the publisher resemble what happens when a homeowner goes into default. Of course, when it comes time to recoup any of the investment, the market price of the set suggests bankruptcy liquidation rates.[6]

Responsible serials acquisition requires a knowledge of current serial prices *and* an awareness of the likely extent of future price increases. In the absence of a crystal ball, surveys of recent price history are the best available tools for estimating future price increases. There are several sources for such information: industry-wide surveys published in the professional literature, the title- and institution-specific history files maintained by many serial vendors, and local library records.

The most frequently used industry surveys are the ALA Price Index of U.S. Periodicals and Serial Services compiled by the Library Materials Price Index Committee of the Resources and Technical Services Division of the American Library Association, published in the mid-April issue of *Library Journal*; B.H. Blackwell's Periodical Price Index, published in the May issue of the *Library Association Record*; and the Faxon Price Index, published less regularly in the *Serials Librarian*.[7] All are generalized indexes, reporting price movement in categories of serial materials rather than specific titles. The ALA index reports only on U.S. publications; the Blackwell and Faxon indexes cover serials from all countries.

While providing useful information highlighting pricing trends in relation to periodical serials in specific subject areas, industry-wide surveys are not necessarily accurate indicators of price trends for the specific titles in the collections of individual libraries.[8] In recent years two developments have made it easier for libraries to track the pricing history of the titles in their collections. The increasing use of local automated serials control systems provides some libraries with the ability to track precise serial pricing and cost information without extensive manual data collection and analysis, and many serial subscription agencies now make historic pricing data on individual titles available to clients on request. It should be noted that most of these approaches track only subscription prices. Libraries which acquire serials through vendors should also monitor related cost elements such as discounts and service charges. This requires tracking of vendor invoices rather than publishers' subscription prices.

Price increases affect all categories of library materials.

> The average price for a U.S. hardcover monograph in 1987 was $35.34—9 percent over the 1986 average of $32.43. In comparison, U.S. periodicals averaged $71.41 per title in 1987, a 9.9 percent increase over the average price of $65.00 in 1986. Adding to this the output of European-based journal publishers, an even larger increase is evident for all serials: $105.00 for a serial in 1987, a 13.4 percent increase over the 1986 average of $93.32.[9]

Library administrators are particularly concerned about significant increases in the cost of expensive serial titles:

> [Libraries] have discovered that since 1986 no more than 10% of their journals consume 50% or more of the serials budget and that as few as 20% of their subscriptions swallow 72-75% of the serials budget.[10]

> Eighty percent of [Louisiana State University's] journals cost less than $100 per title. The average cost of this group is less than $25. The average cost of the most expensive 20% . . . is about $330 per title. To maintain *Gene* ($1,700/22 issues, 1988) from Elsevier, LSU must forego purchasing 66 "low cost" journals or 41 books.[11]

Publishers respond by focusing on the value of the titles under attack:

> Targeting costly titles for cancellation is an understandable, knee-jerk reaction. Yet those expensive journals can be

extremely cost-effective for both the librarian and scientist. Large, international editorial boards for journals such as the *Journal of Chromatography* or *Biochimica et Biophysica Acta* (BBA) provide broad expertise and ensure rigorous standards in refereeing papers. Such journals serve the research community by consolidating results and providing rapid evaluation of papers.[12]

At \$3,626 per year for 1988, the *Journal of Chromatography* seems expensive. But consider: 63 air-delivered issues per year containing 18,500 pages. Each page costs 20 cents; each article about \$1.80.[13]

Library-sponsored surveys of the cost per page or per character approach to serials pricing show a marked difference between the pricing policies of different kinds of publishers. A report prepared for the Association of Research Libraries in 1989 indicates that "the not-for-profit sector charges libraries per page or per character prices one-half to one-twentieth of those charged by comparable commercial publishers".[14]

DUAL PRICING

Concern about the costs of serials publications has renewed awareness of dual pricing practices which result in different subscription rates for libraries in North America and those in other countries. For the same subscriptions, some European publishers currently charge North American libraries as much as 100 percent more than European libraries.[15] Although European publishers are most often targeted, many U.S. publishers follow the same practice when setting rates for non-U.S. subscribers.

A number of publishers make similar distinctions in subscription rates for individuals and libraries, charging higher prices for institutional subscribers. Some libraries seek to reduce costs by placing their subscriptions in the names of individuals. The care that publishers with dual European-North American pricing take to limit lower subscription rates to titles destined only for lower rate areas suggests that, in their eyes, unqualified receipt of lower rates is anything but a gray area of ethics. At least one publisher denies individuals the option of purchasing subscriptions at the individual rate unless the individual's local or institutional library subscribes to the same journal at the higher institutional rate.

Wide swings in the value of the U.S. dollar have contributed to library awareness of the dual pricing issue, exacerbating the discrepancy between prices for U.S. subscribers and those in other countries. The impact of fluctuations in foreign exchange rates is most noticeable in expensive titles—the output of overseas commercial scientific, technical, and medical publishers, and foreign fashion magazines and other glossies. As discussed in Chapter 3, the cost of foreign subscriptions may be further increased by the service charges levied by third-party vendors.

AN ONGOING COMMITMENT

Few libraries place one-time orders for serials; most expect to continue subscribing indefinitely, or at least for a period of several years. The decision to acquire a serial generally entails an ongoing commitment of funds and multiple accessioning, processing, payment, renewal, and auditing transactions. The funding commitment is open-ended in both amount and duration. The amount is unclear because of the need to accommodate price increases, and the duration depends upon staff and user assessments of the extent to which the title contributes to the library's service mission. The direct financial commitment is higher if the decision to enter a current order is accompanied by the purchase of back issues.

Serial publications also require the ongoing allocation of resources for accessioning and auditing. With monograph purchases, an order is fulfilled by the receipt and processing of a single item. Once the item is accessioned, the invoice can be passed for payment. There is a one-time accountability and fiscal obligation. With serials, accountability is long-term and repetitive. Serial subscriptions are paid in advance, a single order encompasses multiple pieces, and the pieces are received over an extended period of time. Accountability requires that the receipt of each piece be monitored and recorded, that missing pieces be identified and claimed, and that claim records be maintained and monitored to ensure that the missing material is supplied. Continuation of supply requires tracking of subscription expiration dates, the development of procedures to coordinate renewals with expirations, and the regular renewal of orders. In addition, most serial acquisitions also entail other continuing nonacquisition expenses such as cataloging and catalog maintenance, binding, and housing the materials.

METHODS OF ACQUIRING SERIALS

Most libraries use a combination of methods for acquiring serials: purchase through subscription agencies and other vendors; purchase direct from publishers; gifts; and the exchange of materials with other institutions.

Subscription agencies and vendors dominate serials acquisitions, handling at least half and, possibly, two-thirds, of the annual serial expenditures of U.S. libraries. Subscription agencies use economies of scale, discounts from publishers, and sophisticated automated systems to provide basic subscription services: order placement and renewal, publisher prepayment, and support for the claiming of missing issues. Beyond these basics, agencies offer a variety of additional services ranging from printed catalogs and customized invoices to online files of serial pricing data, and electronic messaging systems. Although some agencies offer discounts on certain types of publications and services, they usually levy service or handling fees to cover the cost of service provision.

Some serials are not available through vendors, and some librarians do not believe that subscription agencies offer the most effective and economic route for serials acquisitions. In these circumstances materials are ordered direct from publishers, obtained through exchange with other libraries and institutions, or acquired as gifts.

Exchange programs have been particularly popular for the acquisition of serials from the Third World. In recent years exchange has become less common as shrinking library budgets have focussed attention on administrative costs and the equity of the materials exchanged. (Some commentators have suggested that recent political changes may spark a renewed interest in exchange among libraries in eastern Europe, and that U.S. libraries may be receptive to such overtures.) Exchange continues to be important for libraries serving institutions with active publishing programs that attract exchange offers from organizations that publish standard publications in the same field and when institutions refuse to sell their publications and only make them available through exchange.

Unsolicited gifts can be anything but helpful to a library. As with materials received on exchange,

It is well to remember that gift serials are free only until they arrive at the loading dock. At that point, costs begin to accrue as the library begins the long and expensive process of establishing permanent serials records, cataloging, binding, and providing access.[16]

However, a structured program of guided giving can be rewarding, if a library takes care to match the interest of potential donors with its needs and acquisitions options.

PUBLICATION CHARACTERISTICS

When staff are submitting the third claim for an issue of a popular title much beloved by the chairperson of the library board or trying, yet again, to have the correct address recorded on subscriptions for the corporate R&D unit, it may seem far from the truth that:

> The vast majority of publishers . . . make a conscientious effort to publish on time, solve subscriber complaints, and, generally, this side of a natural or technical disaster, function in such a way as to cause no subscriber . . . much pain.[17]

Many of the challenges libraries experience with serials acquisition have their origins in the nature of the serials format and publishers' policies and procedures rather than in the method of acquisition chosen by a library.

THE SERIALS FORMAT

At its most basic, serials acquisition encompasses order placement and renewal, and the receipt of all issues covered by an order. This seemingly simple operation is complicated by the very nature of serial materials: publications issued as successive parts intended to continue indefinitely. It is continuity over time that provides serials with such spectacular opportunities for irregularity, opportunities that they embrace with enthusiasm all too often.

Publishers' Fulfillment Procedures: The ongoing nature of serial publications requires that publishers establish and maintain relatively complex fulfillment procedures. Whether manual or automated, publishers' fulfillment systems typically encompass:

- soliciting subscriptions,
- receiving and processing new orders and renewals,
- monitoring the life cycle of subscriptions,
- producing mailing labels,
- issuing renewal notices/invoices,
- processing claims for missing issues,
- implementing cancellations, and
- producing management reports.

Although efficient fulfillment procedures will not guarantee the problem-free acquisition of serials materials by libraries, inefficient fulfillment systems will guarantee difficulties. The acquisitions problems caused by fulfillment procedures run the gamut from annoying to serious: delays in the activation of orders and the implementation of adjustments such as address changes; inability to accommodate readily multiple copy orders; and failure to record receipt of orders and payments.

Bibliographic Changes: Serial publications may be intended to continue indefinitely, but nobody would suggest that they are supposed to continue without change. The time dimension of the serials format allows for continuing change in practically any element by which a serial might be identified for acquisitions purposes or remembered or referred to by a user. Changes in title, publisher, place of publication, and frequency are common, as are mergers and splits. Each change has the potential to wreak havoc with acquisitions procedures. Failure to recognize changes in title, publisher, or place of publication can result in the unintended duplication of orders and duplicate payments, and changes in frequency can result in the preparation and dispatch of unnecessary claims for missing issues. [The International Standard Serial Number (ISSN) that serves as a unique identifier for serial publications is tied to the title of a serial and will not necessarily reflect changes in publisher, place of publication, or frequency. When there is a significant change in title, a new ISSN is assigned. It is not always possible, however, to track title changes through ISSNs; not all serials receive ISSNs, many libraries and vendors do not use ISSNs, and ISSN assignments often lag behind title changes.]

Publication Irregularities: Although the concept of regularity is not essential to the definition of a serial, it does apply to many types of serial materials, particularly periodical serials. Publishing schedules are not bound by concepts. Irregularities occur frequently. The possibilities include delays in scheduled publication dates, the publication of extra issues, volumes, and special supplements, and combined issues. Any exceptions to expected patterns of publication complicate the acquisitions process causing unnecessary claiming activity, supplemental invoices, and financial irregularities. In turn, these may result in duplicate payments or premature expiration of a subscription.

PERIODICAL SERIALS

Periodical serials—those published on a regular schedule—are usually acquired by subscription, that is, an order paid in advance for a period of one, two, or more years, as the publisher and/or the local financial authority allow. A subscription remains in force until it is either actively cancelled by the library or allowed to lapse by non-renewal at the end of the subscription period. Alternatively, the subscription may be terminated by the death of the publication.

Consumer Magazines: The so-called "popular," "mass-circulation," or "consumer" magazines sold on newsstands and by subscription include general interest news magazines; titles that target general but narrower markets such as those for fashion, shelter, business and finance, and sports; and more tightly focussed special interest and hobby titles.

Consumer magazine publishers are primarily interested in advertising revenues, using circulation figures (audited by agencies such as the Audit Bureau of Circulation) and demographically desirable subscriber profiles to court advertisers. Subscription income is often of secondary importance to circulation figures. Consumer magazines are among the least expensive serials purchased by libraries. Many magazine publishers offer substantial discounts for new subscribers and individuals. Discounts may also be applied to institutional orders placed through subscription agencies, but discounts for institutions tend to be lower than those for individuals. Consumer magazines are popular in libraries. But libraries are not necessarily attractive to magazine publishers, some of whom view library subscriptions as limiting the pool of potential individual subscribers.

There are signs that these attitudes may be changing. On May 8, 1989, the *New York Times* reported that "[f]or the first time in the modern history of general-interest magazine publishing, revenues from subscriptions and newsstand-copy sales exceed revenues from advertisers. . . ." This could result in the reduction of discounts to libraries and individuals. On the other hand, the focus of advertisers' concerns may also be expanding to encompass the concept of "readership"—the number of individuals who see each copy of a magazine—in addition to subscriber demographics. If this trend develops, publishers' attitudes towards library subscriptions might change. Some industry insiders suggest that library exposure could become so important that publishers might offer libraries free subscriptions to popular magazines in return for open shelf display of their titles.

Meanwhile, many of the problems libraries experience with popular magazines arise from publishers' fulfillment procedures, which are shaped to meet the needs of individual subscribers rather than those of libraries. Many publishers contract out subscription management to fulfillment agencies; others have in-house fulfillment departments. The details of both approaches are similar, only the scale is different.

Fulfillment agencies handle titles from multiple publishers, managing all aspects of subscription solicitation, order processing, mailing label production, renewals, cancellations, and claims processing.[18] The larger fulfillment centers are located in Boulder, Colorado; Marion, Ohio; and Des Moines, Iowa. They manage hundreds of titles, make extensive use of automation, and can achieve significant economies of scale. Library subscriptions represent only a small part—1.5 to 2 percent—of fulfillment center business, but generate up to 50 percent of service complaints.

The mailing labels created during order entry are the key to fulfillment operations. In addition to the subscriber name and address, each label contains a unique code created from fulfillment center data and elements from the subscriber name and address. The code serves as the retrieval key for all information relating to a subscription. Most fulfillment centers use a label format that provides only four lines for subscriber name and address data, each line limited to twenty characters. Longer names and addresses are truncated during order entry. Libraries that order direct from publishers and have long addresses may be able to limit delivery problems by submitting orders with truncated names and addresses rather than relying on the arbitrary abbreviation applied by a fulfillment agent's order entry staff.

Labels or label tapes are generated from the orders and sent to the printers producing the magazines. Labels for specific issues are prepared and shipped weeks in advance of the issue publication dates; it is not unusual for mailing labels for a January issue to be shipped in November. The time lag can be greater if a fulfillment center uses offshore keying services for order entry. Such order entry procedures can result in significant delays in the start of new subscriptions and the implementation of changes in existing orders. Typically, there is a lag of six to eight weeks between a fulfillment center's receipt of an order and the subscriber's receipt of the first issue of a monthly periodical.

Publishers sometimes regulate the flow of subscriptions to control the audited circulation figures on which advertising rates are based. Fulfillment centers implement flow control by accelerating or holding back the entry of new orders. Such controls are not usually applied to renewals. These practices, and the normal lag between order submission and receipt of the first issue, can cause problems with library orders that request specific start dates.

Nor are fulfillment centers geared to the management of orders for multiple copies sent to the same or similar addresses. Changes in multiple copy orders during a subscription cycle can be particularly problematic. New copy orders may be added to existing orders, making them multi-year subscriptions, and cancellation requests for selected copies may be interpreted as cancellation of all copies. The tracking of multiple subscriptions may be facilitated if a library uses a slightly different address for each copy, increasing the chances that a unique label code will be assigned to each subscription.

Librarians are all too familiar with the deluge of renewal notices spawned, often months in advance of the expiration of a subscription, by fulfillment centers. Provided that renewals are sent in plenty of time—a minimum of at least six weeks—they are usually processed more smoothly than new orders. Libraries that order direct from publishers may find that renewal processing is facilitated by use of the computer generated renewal notice or a mailing label from the current subscription. Renewal cards with no annotations or changes are handled by automated card readers and do not require human intervention in the renewal process. Publishers' renewal notices for titles ordered through subscription agencies can generally be ignored; renewal of these titles is handled by the agency.

These problems are minor compared to the difficulties libraries experience when claiming missing or replacement copies. Titles distributed by fulfillment houses have the unsavory distinction of being the serials for which libraries most frequently claim missing issues, partly because these are the titles published most frequently—the weeklies and monthlies. One large subscription agency handling orders and claims for all types of serials from hundreds of libraries surveyed the claims for missing issues of periodicals submitted by its clients from March 1982 through May 1983. The 47 titles generating most claims were all handled by a single fulfillment center. On average, 32 percent of the orders for these titles generated a claim. The title claimed most frequently was *Psychology Today* with 1143 claims for 2408 orders, a claim rate of 47.5 percent.

Fulfillment centers rarely handle copies of the titles they manage, and mass market publishers rarely maintain sets of back issues to meet such claims. Publishing runs are finely tuned to the number of subscribers and expected newsstand sales. Overstocks from magazine stands are not returned to the publisher; they are trashed. Non-institutional subscribers rarely claim missing issues or seek replacements for damaged or defective copies. When claims are submitted, the standard response is to extend the subscription to cover an additional issue. These extensions are unacceptable to libraries seeking to meet user requirements for timely access to each issue of a title and to obtain a full set of issues for retention, and can result in confused renewal schedules and overlaps in subscription payments.

Some publishers do provide their fulfillment agents with limited numbers of replacement copies to service library claims. A library can improve its chances of obtaining replacement issues by submitting claims as soon as possible; claiming direct from the publisher rather than channelling claims through a subscription agency; and including a mailing label from a previous issue with the claim.

Controlled Circulation Magazines: Advertising revenues are the primary source of income for controlled circulation publishers who distribute specialty periodicals gratis (and, often, unsolicited) to businesses and individuals qualified by virtue of their trade or professional responsibilities—data center managers, poultry farmers, financial analysts, physicians, metal manufacturers, and others. Controlled circulation publications may not be available for distribution to unqualified individuals who are not part of their intended audience, or to institutions. If broader distribution is supported, a paid subscription is usually required. School, college, and university libraries that would not otherwise qualify for limited distribution publications can sometimes argue for an exception on the grounds that their students are being trained to enter the field served by a specific title.

Commercial STM Publications: Consumer magazines are distinctive because of the problems libraries experience with fulfillment centers that focus on distribution to individuals. In contrast, periodical serials published by commercial scientific, technical, and medical (STM) publishers such as Elsevier, Springer-Verlag, Wiley, and Pergamon are notable because their subscription and distribution procedures are responsive to the needs of libraries. Together with individual practitioners, libraries are the primary market for STM publishers. The STMs regularly exhibit at library shows, make sales and service visits to libraries, and maintain a high visibility in the library community.

Many STM publishers use automated fulfillment systems attuned to the special needs of libraries. The systems support timely responses to current and back issue orders; provide up-to-date subscription records, price data, and publication schedules; ensure prompt issuance of renewal notices; and promote flexibility in accommodating institutional subscriber address requirements. Of all serials publishers, the commercial STMs are most likely to have facilities to accept machine-readable orders from serials subscription agencies; some also provide pricing and other fulfillment data in machine-readable form. Increasingly, STM publishers operate as international publishers, lessening the impact of the domestic/foreign dichotomy that can be a significant factor in the acquisition of other types of serials. However, many commercial STM publishers continue to maintain domestic/foreign distinctions in pricing.

Effective and responsive distribution networks are essential if commercial STM publishers are to maintain their income base, which depends on subscription revenues rather than advertising dollars. Subscription revenues are attracted not by the mass appeal of STM titles, but by the fact that they are *the* preferred publishing medium in the scientific, technical, and medical fields. The journal format offers timely publication and a narrow, in-depth focus more suited to the reporting of original research than the broad survey approach of monograph publishing. The scientific community's emphasis on serial publication is also fuelled by the structure of the academic rewards system, with its emphasis on published contributions to scholarship.

The benefits of the superior STM distribution network sometimes extend to the publications of professional and scholarly associations such as the American Society for Information Science. Lacking the resources to support all aspects of high-quality in-house publishing programs, such associations often sell their journal rights and production and fulfillment functions to STM publishers in return for royalties.

Learned Societies, Associations, and University Presses: The publishing activities of the societies, associations, and university presses that support large publishing programs are not dissimilar to those of commercial STM publishers. Subscriptions furnish a significant part of publishing revenues, but they are often augmented by page charges, which are fees paid by authors or their institutions to defray publication costs. Although associations usually enjoy the status of tax-exempt educational institutions, profit is an important motive in their publishing programs, providing revenues to support membership and professional services.

The scale and structure of association publishing is illustrated by a 1982 study of six journals published by the American Institute of Physics.[19] The journals generated revenues of $6.2 million of which 61 percent came from subscriptions (two-thirds from nonmembers), 33 percent from voluntary page charges, and 2 percent from reprint sales. Advertising, microform sales, back issue sales, and royalties each generated 1 percent of journal income. The threats to these revenues are also demonstrated: from 1970 to 1982, subscriptions declined by 28 percent.

Libraries which require substantial coverage of the publications of associations and societies can sometimes acquire them at a discount by taking out individual or institutional memberships. [Any library that acquires a number of serials from a single publisher of any kind, but particularly learned and not-for-profit publishers, should discuss the possibility of discounts and consolidated invoices for titles ordered directly from the publisher.] Such discounts more often apply to monographs and non-periodical serials than to periodicals. While some associations offer this opportunity, others consider it unethical; some associations distribute their publications only to members. Like subscriptions, memberships require advance payment. Libraries that maintain memberships often assign responsibility for membership tracking and renewal to the serials department. Memberships may save money or offer access to materials not otherwise available; however, they do not reduce the requirement for monitoring and recording receipt of the titles covered by the membership.

Not all societies, associations, and groups have publication programs that rival those of large commercial publishers in scale and efficiency. Many put together journals and newsletters using volunteer labor rather than a salaried editorial staff and are poorly organized to support the timely distribution of materials to their own members, let alone to handle subscription payments, renewal notices, mailing lists, and claims from nonmembers. The less formal the publication, the more likely that there will be problems. Publishing irregularities are particularly common with the proceedings and papers of annual meetings.

Government Publications: If the successful pursuit of government publications often requires the sleuthing talents of Sherlock Holmes, the skills of a platoon of Sherlock Holmeses are required to track government serials! And, according to some estimates, 70 to 80 percent of all government publications are serials.[20] There are no easy solutions. Success depends upon effort, knowledge and experience, and a sensitivity to, and tolerance for, the peculiarities of the publications required by a specific library. Libraries with large collections of government publications often organize acquisitions so that all government publications—serials and nonserials— are handled by staff specialists. This allows concentration and full use of expertise and acquisitions resources such as bibliographies and files of publisher and agency data. Such an arrangement also bypasses the problems of definition entailed in categorizing government publications as either serial or non-serial.

The three major challenges in developing and maintaining collections of government serials are: finding out about the existence of specific titles and their availability; obtaining a steady supply of the materials; and tracking frequent changes in titles and/ or the names of issuing bodies. These challenges apply with varying degrees of intensity to serials published by local, state/provincial, national, and international governments.

Finding out about the serials published by national and state governments requires consulting:

> . . . a variety of accessions lists and sales catalogues because the central government does not provide a complete listing. It is common practice for government departments themselves to publish some if not all of their publications, so the general catalogues issued by the government printer are never complete, and individual ministries/departments may fail to issue their own catalogues. . . . A further problem arises with "restricted circulation" and "not for sale" items; these frequently pass unrecorded and may not even be permanently filed by the issuing department.[21]

The situation is no better for the serials of intergovernmental organizations, only 14 percent of which publish current bibliographies, and some of these infrequently.[22] Information about the publications of local governments is even less readily available, and acquisition of these materials relies heavily on local contacts and collecting activities.

Many North American libraries acquire national and state government publications through depository programs. While such programs relieve libraries of the cost of purchasing the materials, they must still meet the costs entailed in receiving, processing, and storing them. In recent years, increasing privatization of government publishing has added to library costs as titles previously available on deposit become available only on a subscription basis.

Few general subscription agencies are equipped to handle any but the most prominent domestic and international government publications; however, a number of specialist vendors focus on government publications.[23] Some commercial publishers offer alternatives for the acquisition of government publications, often republishing them in microformat in association with abstracting and indexing access tools.

Subscription agency coverage of government serials from the Third World is generally poor. Acquisition of these materials relies heavily upon individual efforts, cooperative acquisitions projects by institutions with representatives in these areas, contacts with book dealers in the countries of interest, and unstable deposit and exchange relationships.

Serial Services: Serials services are periodical publications that revise, cumulate, abstract, or index information in a specific field on a regular basis by means of new or replacement issues, pages, or cards. They are of particular significance in business, administration, law, and other social sciences. The materials may be published frequently, sometimes weekly or daily, often in loose-leaf format. Payment is required in advance, annually or every two years. Most of the large publishers of specialized serials services such as Westlaw, Commerce Clearing House, Standard and Poor's, and Prentice-Hall, have field agents or regional representatives who visit libraries to solicit renewals and promote new services. Since representatives receive a commission on orders, most prefer that libraries deal directly with them instead of with the home office.

Newspapers: Newspaper publishers focus on the direct distribution of a highly perishable commodity. Their revenues depend upon advertisers attracted by the prospect of timely, in-depth circulation by home or office delivery and newsstand sales in a localized area. Few newspaper publishers assign great importance to mail subscriptions, which are expensive and labor intensive to service.

> Invoices are often mailed . . . so late in a subscription period that no library could pay promptly enough to prevent gaps in service. [Because of their frequency of publication, the] grace

period for newspaper deliveries at the end of a subscription is extremely brief, and those insignificant slips of paper that often constitute renewal notices are easily missed.[24]

There are exceptions. Newspapers such as the *Wall Street Journal* provide toll-free subscriber help numbers and contract with delivery services for distribution in major metropolitan areas.

Libraries with mail subscriptions to out-of-town or national newspapers frequently experience difficulty with the timeliness of supply and receipt of the required edition. Subscription rates vary with postal zone charges and coverage. (weekly or Sundays-only), and are subject to frequent change. Metropolitan newspapers and those with national coverage are issued in multiple editions, the contents of which vary by region and time of day. The choice of edition can be problematic for titles with national coverage. Should the library acquire the regional edition that focusses on the local area, the edition that is indexed in a specific abstracting and indexing service, or both?

Many corporate and special libraries are responsible for the distribution of multiple copies of local, regional, and national newspapers within their institutions. The titles in question may be general—the *Wall Street Journal* or *New York Times*—or specialist—*Energy Daily*. Although not usually regarded as a major focus of library activities, the smooth distribution of newspapers can have a major impact on management's perceptions of the quality and value of library service. When this is a critical factor in library assessment, many libraries place permanent supply orders with local specialized newspaper distributors who handle newsstand supply of these titles, rather than relying on routine mail subscriptions.

Microform Editions of Newspapers, Periodicals, and Other Serials: Many libraries purchase microform editions of newspapers and periodicals. This is frequently the most convenient way of obtaining substantial backsets and can be an attractive and economic alternative to the binding and storage costs entailed in retaining the hard-copy version of a title. The superior archival characteristics of microform are of importance to libraries developing research collections.

A decision to acquire microforms involves a range of technical considerations. Microform publishers may offer choices in relation to microformat (fiche, roll-film, and more unusual formats such as micro-cards and other micro-opaque media); reduction ratio, (48X or 24X fiche, 16 or 35 mm film, 80 to 150X ultrafiche, etc.);

and film medium, (silver halide, diazo, or vesicular). Or, a publisher may offer no choice at all, providing, for example, only 35 mm silver halide roll-film copy for a specific title. The availability and cost of reader/printers for the chosen media must also be considered.

Micropublishing is essentially republishing. Materials are filmed and dispatched after the publication and distribution of the hard copy version. In the United States, University Microfilms International (UMI) is the dominant publisher of newspapers and journals on microfilm. The company has exclusive micropublication rights to more than 16,000 journals and 7,000 newspapers, including the *Wall Street Journal* and the *New York Times*. UMI handles both domestic and foreign titles. It offers 24X fiche and 35mm and 16mm roll-film formats in 18X reduction. Vesicular stock is used for current year subscriptions, silver halide for backsets. [The consensus is that silver halide has greater archival stability than diazo stock. The jury is still out on vesicular film, but it is thought to be durable.] Orders must be placed direct; UMI does not accept orders from subscription agencies.

A number of other companies specialize in microfilming current serials, and some serials publishers handle their own microfilming. Information on the availability of microform versions of current serials is usually found (often in very small print) in the hard copy editions. Publishers who retain responsibility for both printed and microform editions of their titles sometimes offer discounts for subscriptions to both editions of a title.

The frequency with which microform editions of current print publications are issued varies according to demand and publishers' schedules. For example, UMI distributes microforms of high-demand daily newspapers on a monthly schedule; less popular dailies are issued annually. Microrepublishers experience delays in the availability of materials similar to those encountered by libraries: lags in print publication schedules, delays caused by the need to replace damaged copies, and difficulties in assembling complete sets of the material to be filmed. In filming, pages or issues of a title can be omitted. Libraries which rely on microform editions of newspapers for research find it advisable to check each delivery to ensure that no issues have been missed.

Microrepublishing of current serials is not confined to commercial enterprises and individual publishers. Many libraries microfilm current materials of local or special interest, and make copies of these films available for purchase. It is difficult, however, to obtain information on the availability of such materials. Moreover, publishing schedules are often irregular, and copyright concerns can inhibit distribution of the film to other libraries.

Filming of non-current, retrospective serials is the major focus of not-for-profit institutional activity, fuelled by the desire to make rare materials more widely available or, increasingly, to ensure the long-term preservation of titles published on non-archival paper stock. Commercial companies are also active in this arena, producing sets of serials or including serials titles in more broadly based collections of monograph and serials resources. Obtaining information on the availability of such materials can be a major headache. This problem increasingly concerns librarians involved in preservation microfilming, but is unlikely to be amenable to a quick solution. Librarians wishing to locate microform editions of non-current serials have to rely on the data bases of bibliographic utilities such as OCLC and RLIN, individual subject and project catalogs, and word-of-mouth.

Packaged Periodicals: As indicated in the discussion of government publications, there are often alternative means of acquiring materials covered by abstracting and indexing (A&I) services. A number of them are repackaged by the A&I producers and made available in compact formats. Initially produced in microform, such compilations are now becoming available on CD-ROM and online services as machine-searchable ASCII files or electronically scanned image facsimiles of the print publications.

ERIC and NTIS reports are available in microform, as are the government publications indexed by the Congressional Information Service. Information Access Company (IAC) markets microfilm of the journal articles covered by its indexes as integrated products. Articles from different sources are mingled on roll film distributed every two weeks. IAC also publishes printed index and contents guides to provide direct, index-independent access to the filmed materials. Other vendors, such as UMI, offer discounted subscriptions to individual microform titles purchased with their A&I products.

UMI is experimenting with the distribution of CD-ROMs containing scanned images of the documents covered by its A&I services. [The UMI products carry both a subscription price and a per page charge for hard-copy prints generated from the files. This pricing mechanism represents a compromise between publishers' concerns that electronic distribution will erode hard-copy subscription revenues, and UMI's need to price its products at a level that will appeal to the market. Electronic publishers find that serials publishers who rely on subscription income to support their publications are more cautious about making them available in non-print formats than are publishers whose revenues are based on income from advertising.] Document image facsimiles do not support word-by-word text searching. Such access requires use of ASCII coded machine-readable text—the format used in online full-text periodical and newspaper data bases. A number of producers are experimenting with the publication on CD-ROM of full-text, machine-searchable files of the materials covered by their A&I products.

Little Magazines and Alternative Publications: Little magazines—noncommercial literary magazines—and alternative, grass-roots, and underground publications share erratic publication schedules and idiosyncratic purchasing requirements. Such materials are rarely available through subscription agencies or other vendors, and require labor intensive acquisitions procedures in libraries.

The problems encountered by libraries seeking to develop and maintain collections of alternative serials materials are illustrated by the attitudes found among editors of little magazines:

> . . . little magazine editors frequently are best dealt with on a one-to-one, personal basis. His magazine may be an editor's consuming interest and he may resent the idea that some would consider it just another serial to be ordered.[25]

> Those for whom invoices in quadruplicate are standard may be surprised to find that some editors resent such inconveniences or are simply unprepared to deal with them. The business of art is art, not business.[26]

Additional problems can arise with serials from publishers and organizations that espouse non-mainstream political or social views. In some cases, such materials can only be obtained through membership subscriptions. It can be difficult to explain the need for a library to hold membership in such organizations. Other groups may be reluctant to make their publications available to certain libraries, fearing that this will subject them to government scrutiny. Such issues, which can be major barriers when collecting domestic materials, are exacerbated when attempting to collect foreign publications.

Foreign Titles: The acquisitions peculiarities of different types of periodical serials are enhanced when a library is dealing with materials published in another country. At the simplest level, crossing national boundaries involves foreign currency transactions, fluctuating currency rates, and complex and expensive procedures to obtain foreign currency drafts. At the next level, language differences increase the complexity of the order-payment-maintenance cycle. Cultural differences may impose additional barriers. None of these factors pose significant problems for North American libraries seeking mainstream titles published in the developed world. Such titles can be ordered direct, obtained through North American or European agencies, or acquired through exchange.

Subscription agencies follow a variety of practices in calculating and billing foreign exchange transactions, and in applying service charges for foreign titles. A library seeking to acquire a significant amount of foreign material through a subscription agency should evaluate the services of several competing vendors. In some circumstances European agencies offer lower cost service than their U.S. counterparts.

Although not widely publicized, many subscription agencies channel their orders for limited interest or regional foreign titles through foreign agencies. This approach may be dictated by government policy or the ordering requirements of specific publishers. It is not unusual for competing agencies to use the same foreign agent.

When assessing a vendor's ability to provide service for foreign titles, libraries need to probe beneath the rhetoric of corporate advertising. It is fashionable for larger agencies to stress their international offices and affiliations. Such connections do not of themselves guarantee better, faster, or less expensive service. Not that agency advertising is at fault; given the opportunity, librarians are not reluctant to jump to their own conclusions, often based on false assumptions. For example, it is easy to assume that a North American vendor with an automated system linked to the system of an affiliate in Europe will use the linkage to facilitate service to clients in North America. Such assumptions need to be identified and verified. The automated linkage may serve only to provide information on North American titles to European clients.

Third World Titles: Greater persistence is required if a library wishes to obtain alternative publications from foreign countries, or has a serials collection with a focus on material from Asia, Africa, South America, or the Soviet block. In addition to the language and currency complications that attend all international transactions, Third World and developing countries often experience social and economic conditions which frustrate attempts to distribute serials and cause serials publishing itself to be sporadic and uncertain.

Political upheavals and nonviolent political change impact heavily upon publishing and distribution.

Although large serials subscription agencies emphasize the international scope of their activities, often claiming to be able to handle subscriptions to serials of all types published in all countries,

> [e]xperience suggests that their idea of international rarely extends beyond Europe and North America. The few Asian and African titles listed in their catalogues . . . tend to be mostly in science and technology. Some will only accept orders for titles listed in their catalogues. This leaves a large number to be acquired by other means and defeats one of the main reasons for using a serials agent, i.e., to channel payments, claims, and correspondence through one intermediary.[27]

Research libraries with a strong interest in serials publications from the Third World have experimented with a variety of acquisition methods, none of which offers a total solution. Local subscription agencies are not well-established, and many libraries try to identify reliable local book vendors to handle their serials needs. Recommendations from other libraries with similar area interests can be a valuable source of leads. If an appropriate source is identified, some libraries set up blanket orders for serials. [Under a blanket order, a library defines the subjects and/or publishers of interest and indicates the amount of money it wishes to allocate to such materials. The actual selection of titles is made by the agency.] Blanket orders for serials are not a universal success. Libraries may experience difficulty in communicating the scope of their interests, and agents frequently have problems in ensuring a regular supply once the choice of serials has been made. In the words of a librarian who has experimented with blanket orders for serials from Africa and Asia: "All too often it seems as if the supplier has simply despatched whatever happened to be lying around when he was packing up a parcel."[28] In some countries it is not possible to place subscriptions direct with publishers. For example, Bangladesh serials, except for newspapers, can be exported only by registered dealers.

Many libraries have sought to overcome the acquisitions barriers associated with foreign serials, particularly those from Third World countries, by establishing exchange programs with foreign institutions. The effectiveness of this approach varies from exchange to exchange. In some cases they work very well, in others their only effect is to cause problems and expense for both partners.

One of the most effective but expensive methods of acquiring publications from Third World countries is to establish a local purchasing office in the region of interest, staffed with knowledge-able personnel with the resources to make regular visits to government departments, universities, and institutions of all kinds. Such programs are usually developed under the auspices of major research libraries.

NON-PERIODICAL SERIALS

Many of the acquisitions peculiarities of periodical serials are shared by non-periodical serials which also have idiosyncracies of their own. Publishers of non-periodical serials follow a wide variety of ordering and pricing policies; the variations are much greater than among periodical serials. Both libraries and vendors experience problems in ensuring a steady and reliable supply of non-periodical serials.

Terminology and definition can cause significant communications problems when people from different backgrounds or organizations attempt to discuss the acquisition of non-periodical serials. There is little agreement and even less precision as to what constitutes a non-periodical serial, and publishers, vendors, and librarians all use different, but similar and related terms to describe payment and ordering procedures.

Non-periodical serials rarely require prepayment. They are usually billed like monographs, an invoice being issued with the item, or shortly after its dispatch. Individual volumes can be ordered singly like books, or an order can be placed for all volumes in a series or continuation. Librarians refer to such ongoing orders as "standing orders"; many vendors describe them as "automatic renewal" or "'til forbid" orders. When a standing order is in force, supply is continuous until the order is cancelled. To prevent duplicates, a library that maintains standing orders for monographs in series and uses vendor approval plans for monograph acquisitions should provide its approval plan vendors with a full list of the titles for which standing orders are maintained.

[In contrast, orders for periodical serials are usually placed as subscriptions for a finite period or a specific number of issues. Subscriptions require positive renewal action to activate the order for another term. Some vendors will accept standing orders for periodical serials as well as for non-periodical serials, and some European agencies treat all periodical subscriptions as standing orders. Standing orders for periodical serials operate the same way as those for non-periodical serials: they are automatically renewed until the library cancels them.]

Non-periodical serials include monographs in series, multivolume sets, and continuations. Monographs in series are hybrid publications that are both serials and not serials. Each volume stands alone as a book and can be purchased and read as a book without reference to any other volume in the series. However, the numbering and series title frequently result in their being treated as serials in libraries. Continuations or sets are published over a period of years, but have a planned conclusion. They are not generally regarded as true serials but are frequently treated as such in library acquisitions and accessioning.

Individual volumes of non-periodical serials may be published on a regular schedule, or irregularly. The volumes do not necessarily appear in numerical sequence, and some series are unnumbered. Titles obtained on standing order need to be carefully monitored to ensure that the order is actually fulfilled and that no volumes are missed. In addition to uncertainties over publication schedules (e.g., Will a volume be published this year? How many volumes will be published this year?), the cost of individual volumes may vary, and prices often cannot be determined in advance of publication. Hence, it can be difficult to anticipate the financial resources required to meet standing order commitments in any given year.

The proceedings of "floating" international conferences such as the International Geographic Congress illustrate some of the difficulties inherent in acquiring non-periodical serials. Such conferences are usually held once every four or five years, with a different country hosting the meeting each time. The papers or proceedings are usually published in the language of the host country, often as hardcover monographs, but sometimes as issues of existing periodicals. Each congress is handled by a different publisher.

Most North American subscription agencies will handle orders for non-periodical serials. However, many libraries find their services inadequate and prefer to use book vendors for the acquisition of such titles. The bibliographic and publishing data book dealers provide for non-periodical serials is often more responsive than that provided by subscription agencies, and discounts may be higher. Generally, North American subscription agencies have fewer links to the book trade than do European agencies, which appear to experience less difficulty in handling orders for non-periodical serials.

SERIALS IN ELECTRONIC FORMATS

During the 1980s options for the publication and distribution of serials in electronic format matured. At present, the majority of electronic publications are machine-readable: they present text that can be searched, word by word, by appropriate software. Serials in this format may be distributed on floppy disk, magnetic tape, or CD-ROM, all of which can be mounted on computers at the local library site. Other publishers have chosen not to distribute copies of their machine-readable files, but to load them on central computers and provide online access through telecommunications linkages.

The most widely publicized format for the publication of machine-readable serials is CD-ROM, and the type of serials most often published on CD-ROM are abstracting and indexing services. CD-ROM is also popular for the publication of statistics and directories and, increasingly, for the full text of journals and newspapers.

Machine-readable files are an attractive alternative to print for many serials, earning accolades for ease of use, immediacy, and a depth of access superior to that offered by parallel print products. This is not the place to debate the pros and cons of the electronic formats. However, concerns include: cost, lack of standardized retrieval hardware and software, technological obsolescence, and the provision of ongoing access to materials published in electronic format.

Acquisitions procedures vary. While some CD-ROM titles are available through subscription agencies, others must be purchased direct from the publisher. In some cases, the purchase may in fact be a conditional lease or rental that requires the return of all materials if a subscription is not renewed, rather than outright ownership.

As technologies develop to support simultaneous access to a single CD-ROM from multiple local and remote workstations, purchase or lease are further complicated by licensing considerations. Publishers are experimenting with a variety of licensing methods. Many price their products according to the number of workstations able to gain simultaneous access to the file; others will not make their products available for use on CD-ROM networks. Libraries which have pioneered CD-ROM networking report that the negotiation and maintenance of licensing agreements for CD-ROM is time-consuming and ongoing, often requiring adjustments as publishers change their policies or libraries expand the capabilities of their networks. Publishers willing to license their products for use in single-building networks may not be prepared to allow access on networks that encompass multiple buildings; others that allow access through hard-wired networks may not permit remote access by dial-in users.

The immense storage capacities of optical media have led to experiments with the capture and distribution of digitized images of hard-copy documents. Materials in this format are storage-intensive but can be reconstituted into facsimiles of printed document pages, complete with illustrations and graphs. They are not, however, machine-readable any more than the images on microfilm are machine-readable. Such image files can be accessed only through index terms or codes assigned during imaging.

From the point of view of serials acquisitions, one of the most challenging format is electronic mail, the "fugitive" medium of the information age, now being joined by facsimile. Several major newspapers offer fax editions, and the technology is also being used for the rapid distribution of scientific information. The results of the Utah cold fusion experiments were widely distributed by fax two months before they were reported in the traditional print literature.[29]

There are several schools of thought on the likely effects of electronic publishing on the activities of traditional serials vendors. Some observers believe that when no physical item is involved, the electronic formats will be distributed without agency intervention either direct from publishers to subscribers or through third-party distributors with experience in data base services. Current licensing developments would also appear to support this direct contact scenario for the distribution of CD-ROM and machine-readable tapes, requiring direct negotiation of licensing agreements between publisher and purchaser. Others view the formats as offering a natural fit with the services traditionally provided by subscription agencies such as facilitating access between libraries and publishers.

SERIALS: THE NEXT DECADE

Despite the popularity of predictions of the coming of a paperless society and the demise of the print media, the authors believe that it is unlikely that any startling changes in serials publishing will occur in the next decade. We expect current trends to continue: growth in the number of titles published in both traditional and electronic formats; across-the-board price increases with the greatest escalation in expensive titles; and a steady demand for serial materials in libraries coupled with increasing library sensitivity to serial costs.

Libraries may have opportunities to realize savings on consumer magazines if publishers promote the concept of readership or "exposure counts" as an adjunct to subscriber demographics for attracting advertising. While the current focus on the cost of STM serials from commercial publishers has introduced a chill into the relationship between publishers and libraries, we regard this as a temporary freeze as libraries are a primary market for these materials. Indeed, some commercial publishers with an academic focus appear to be taking advantage of the exposure they are receiving in the pricing debate by increasing their sales representation to maintain closer contact with major library accounts. This could result in more libraries placing their orders direct rather than through subscription agencies or other vendors, particularly in the case of libraries that purchase a substantial number of titles from a single publisher.

In all areas of serials publishing, economic and management pressures are likely to cause closer scrutiny of the relationship between publishing runs and sales. As a result, the number of single issues to fill libraries' claims for missing issues will diminish. The impact of such reductions may be softened by the widespread availability of facsimile and electronic mail, which would facilitate prompt submission of claims and other communications between libraries, vendors, and publishers.

Library concern over serial prices will continue. More sophisticated data will become available as serials suppliers and automated serial systems vendors further refine the price tracking capabilities of their systems. Organizations such as the Association of Research Libraries and individual academic and research libraries will continue to promote research into the mechanics and economics of scholarly communication and to enlist the scholarly and funding communities in the fight to control price increases. These programs are of interest to libraries of all types since the research and educational efforts of academic libraries are readily transferable to other library settings.

It is unlikely that a fairy godmother will emerge to rescue libraries from the serial cost dilemma. Library administrators and serials managers will be forced to find workable solutions that rely on factors other than miraculous infusions of funding.[30] We believe that careful management of the acquisitions process provides one such solution.

2 SUBSCRIPTION AGENCIES

United States libraries will spend more than $1 billion on serials in 1990. More than half of this will be channeled through serials subscription agencies, the single most common method of serials acquisition by libraries.

Serials subscription agencies are commercial service organizations that process serial orders and renewals for libraries, corporate and institutional procurement offices, and individuals. They perform the clerical procedures associated with dealing with multiple publishers and reduce the number of invoices, payments, and sources to be handled by libraries. Subscription agencies place new and renewal orders with publishers, forwarding the appropriate payments with the orders (often in advance of receipt of payment from the client). They maintain detailed payment and order records and issue each client a single consolidated invoice covering orders to multiple publishers. Agencies also serve as clearinghouses for contact between libraries and publishers; they provide bibliographic and pricing information, handle subscription problems, and forward claims for missing issues.

Some publishers give agencies discounts—subscription rates lower than the list price charged to libraries that place orders direct. Until the 1960s, the difference between the list price agencies billed their clients and the discount price they remitted to publishers covered agency costs. In some cases, the differential was sufficient to meet agency costs *and* to allow agents to pass on some of the discount to libraries. The practice is similar to that followed by monograph publishers and book wholesalers and jobbers; however, discounts for serials are lower than those for monographs. The percentage discounts publishers offer for serials have been declining since the mid-sixties.

The confluence of reduced discounts and increased costs led to the introduction of service charges in the mid-1960s. Service charges or handling fees fill the gap between agency costs and revenues from publisher discounts. By the 1980s, service charges were the rule rather than the exception. The exception became the fact that some agencies continued to provide discounts or service at no fee to libraries with lists containing a high proportion of heavily discounted consumer magazines or other titles on which publishers provide high dollar discounts to agencies. Agency management of subscriptions at a discount or no service fee usually applied only to school libraries and smaller public libraries. In the second half of the 1980s, agency competition combined with the escalating cost of foreign commercial publications to extend the concept of subscription management with no service fee to cover many of the commercial STM publications acquired by academic, research, and special libraries. [Although the percentage discount publishers offer agencies on such publications may have decreased, price increases provide agencies with significant revenues. For example, a ten percent discount on a title with a list price of $150 yields $15. If the price of the journal increases to $300 and the discount percentage is reduced to seven percent, the yield on the title increases to $21.]

In North America, agency discounts and service charges are typically within ten percent of the list price of a library's subscriptions. Discounts and service charges can be negotiated. Some agencies voluntarily provide discounts or limit service charges, establishing a dollar ceiling on the charge levied against any one title or offering reduced service charges to clients who pay their invoices in advance. In other situations, negotiation must be initiated by the library.

Subscription agency discounts and service charges impact different types of libraries in different ways. School libraries and small to medium-sized public libraries with collections rich in mass-market titles regularly receive discounts. Such opportunities are rarely available on the complete lists of larger public libraries, colleges and universities, and business, law, medical, or government libraries. These libraries may, however, obtain discounts on popular magazines and foreign commercial publications if they segment their lists and separate out these titles for special treatment.

WHY USE AN AGENCY?

Most librarians believe that it is to the benefit of all but the smallest library to use a subscription agency instead of placing orders directly with publishers. The consensus is overwhelming (but not unanimous).[31] The benefits most frequently identified are reductions in library workloads and agent expertise in dealing with publishers:

> Instead of entering orders with hundreds or even thousands of individual publishers, the library uses one agent. This means a single order, a single invoice, a single payment, and a single source of most, if not all, periodicals. Furthermore, the agent renews subscriptions, offers a variety of purchasing plans, handles claims for missing or slow material, and proportionately offers a number of other services. . .[32]

Some of the chief advantages of the subscription agent's service are: the library reduces paperwork, with a subsequent savings in time and money; the agent knows best how to deal with the peculiarities of different publishers; the agent can more easily deal with foreign currency, shipping delays, and erratic foreign service; and the agency can automatically take care of renewals and claims.[33]

. . . payment of the agent's service charge is a much more visible expense than the cost of the staff hours involved in ordering, renewing, and processing serial invoices and the cost of the postage involved in these transactions with many different publishers. The value received for a subscription agent's services is, in large part, dependent upon the cost of the library's serials labor force. . . . For many large libraries, a $50,000 service charge paid for handling $1 million worth of serials would not come close to buying enough in-house staff to handle subscriptions as expeditiously and successfully as can be done by subscription agents, even if funds could be diverted to personnel.[34]

. . . the major advantages of using a basic subscription handling service are savings in staff work hours needed for ordering and invoice processing and . . . more rapid payment to publishers. Libraries with a small number of serials and the ability to dispatch a check quickly may operate relatively efficiently without a subscription agent, although such libraries often do not have the necessary tools and resources to determine current publisher addresses and price information.[35]

Despite the consensus, it can be difficult to find precise documentation of the extent of the savings that accrue to libraries using subscription agencies. Such detail can be useful when explaining subscription agency services to library boards, upper management, or business managers.

The University of Michigan Library performed a retrospective study of ordering patterns and workloads for purchasing domestic monographs.[36] The study compared statistics on orders placed direct with publishers and those placed with vendors. Staff concluded that the results "vividly portray the vendor as the less expensive source for fulfilling the orders of a large academic library." Many of the findings are relevant to the handling of serials subscriptions, in universities and other medium to large libraries, and libraries with either manual or automated systems.

Among the time, labor, and money savings attributed to the use of vendors in the Michigan study were:

- Time saved by not having to look up, transcribe, and maintain publisher addresses and, in an automated environment, concomitant savings in data entry, computer storage requirements, and system access time.

> Because we are using vendors, the storage capacity of our system does not need space for hundreds of publisher addresses. (page 65)

- Labor savings in operations such as envelope stuffing and sealing when orders are sent to a single supplier. [In serials operations, the same procedures are more relevant to the handling of claims for missing issues.]:

> It takes 19 seconds to place one order in an envelope. If seven orders are stuffed in one envelope the average time per order is reduced to 7.8 seconds. The linear relationship is interrupted at eight slips because seven represents the maximum number of slips that can be held in a single envelope. This occurs again at 15 but not at 22 since large manilla envelopes are used for batches of this size. (page 59)

And:

> Once envelopes are stuffed, they must be sealed which again reinforces the economy of batched handling. The small white envelopes holding one to seven order slips take an average of 4.2 seconds to seal regardless of how many items they contain. The larger brown envelopes require some 15 seconds for sealing but they might hold as many as 30 or 40 slips so the unit time is considerably reduced. (page 59)

- Savings in postal charges:

> Over and above the processing time . . . additional postage costs are incurred by sending out many individual slips as opposed to several batched orders. Single slips mailed to domestic vendors require postage in the amount of 22 cents, but batches of 25 or 30 slips can be mailed to a vendor for 56 cents. (page 59)

- Savings in the processing of multiple line invoices compared to single line invoices:

    > . . .bill paying procedures include entering payment information in the automated acquisitions system, photocopying invoices, batching copies to be forwarded to the University central accounting office, and other related record-keeping activities. Studies were made comparing processing time for one invoice of 50 line items with 50 invoices with one line item each . . . it took 160 minutes and 175 minutes to process the 50 one-line item invoices. In marked contrast, the times recorded for the one 50-line invoices were 24 and 35 minutes respectively. (page 61)

    > The payment process is clearly and dramatically affected by the number of receipts from a specific source. The review of this process is enough to convince me that ordering directly from a publisher is a clear waste of staff time and energy. (page 64)

And, a related benefit for libraries with cumbersome financial procedures:

> Publishers sometimes require advanced payment and fulfilling this requirement, when large university processes are taken into account, can be lengthy and cumbersome. (page 65)

- Overall, the study was unequivocal on the benefits of using vendors:

    > If we were to use publishers instead of vendors, we would need more than twice the staff to perform the functions reviewed in the study. In no instance did we realize a staff saving by ordering from the publisher. (page 65)

And,

> By saving staff costs, we are also making a savings in other ways. Because we need less staff, we need less space to house the staff. Supplies and equipment needs are also reduced proportionally. Our automated systems costs are less because we have need for only a limited number of terminals for the staff. (page 65)

The experience of the British Library Document Supply Centre (BLDSC) confirms the Michigan study.[37] The BLDSC receives some 53,000 current serials, over 74 percent of which (more than 40,000 titles) are purchased through agents, with only three percent being obtained directly from publishers. The rest are obtained through gift and exchange. BLDSC uses 13 different agents in various countries. Direct purchase takes place only when the material cannot be obtained through an agent. BLDSC management is emphatic about the benefits it realizes from using serials subscription agencies:

> The main reason for BLDSC's continued patronage of subscription agents can be summed up in two words: convenience and cost-effectiveness. The convenience of using agents leads to staff savings, which result—if the agents are efficient—in cost-effectiveness. (page 128)

The Serials Acquisition Section at BLDSC handles the day-to-day work of ordering serials, sending claims, and dealing with the paperwork and correspondence relating to the serials collection. Comparison of the staffing levels and work loads in the unit illustrates the advantages of using subscription agencies:

> Approximately 8,000 titles acquired through agents can be handled by one member of BLDSC staff, whereas because much letter-writing becomes necessary when dealing with numerous individual publishers, each of which operates in a slightly different way, fewer than 2,000 titles purchased directly from publishers fully occupies one member of staff. (page 128)

In evaluating these figures, it should be noted that subscription agencies are best able to handle the materials that cause libraries the fewest problems; the titles that BLDSC orders direct are likely to be less routine than those available through agencies. BLDSC also believes that agencies:

> . . .can provide a level of expertise not possessed by library personnel. Agents are frequently in direct contact with publishers and, as a result, amass a great deal of knowledge about publisher whims and procedures. Agents learn quickly which publishers demand prepayment and which have specific ordering requirements; they know when subscription periods can and cannot start; and they usually maintain up-to-date

files of publishers' addresses or details of distribution centers, where relevant. Agents can offer expertise in a wide variety of languages, especially if the company is based in the appropriate country, e.g. Japan or Poland, and can communicate directly with publishers in their respective languages. Detailed knowledge of national or local publishing practices can also prove a valuable asset. (pages 129-130)

Again, libraries should be cautious when assigning weight to this factor. It will be of limited significance if a library's list is composed primarily of titles from mainstream international, domestic, or European publishers.

BASIC AGENCY SERVICES

Serials subscription agencies offer a wide range of products and services. In deciding whether to use a subscription agency, which subscription agency/agencies to use, and which products and services to contract for, a library must first determine its serials supply needs, define its service priorities, and evaluate the fit between these requirements and the services offered by agencies. If there is an appropriate match between library needs and available services, the library then needs to analyze the relative costs and benefits of in-house acquisition versus acquisition through vendors.

All subscription agencies offer the same basic services. This fact is often obscured by the marketing stances agencies use to distinguish themselves from their competitors, variously emphasizing factors such as:

- size—large being equated with market success and hence good service and/or responsiveness, small with personalized service;
- number of years in business—longevity implying expertise and track record;
- specialization—being attuned to the special needs of specific market segments such as medical libraries, law libraries, corporate libraries, academic libraries, school libraries, etc.;
- ownership—American companies invoking patriotism and international affiliations suggesting greater facility in handling non-U.S. material; and
- the range and sophistication of automated support services—bigger or more implying better.

In specific situations each of these claims may be valid and may have an impact upon the quality of service a library receives from an agency. However, the rhetoric can be confusing. As an antidote, it can be useful to consider what services are essential to effective agency management of a library's serials acquisitions.

In 1972, Greenfield defined the basic functions of subscription management as:

1. Accurate, prompt placement of new orders.
2. Speedy and vigorous attention to claims and adjustments.
3. Timely renewal of expiring subscriptions.[38]

These functions apply equally to subscription agencies *and* direct serials acquisitions by libraries. If subscription agencies are to be an effective alternative to ordering direct from publishers, they must also:

4. Reduce the expenditure of library resources on subscription placement, renewal, and fulfillment.

The accurate placement of orders requires that an agent:

• identify the titles requested by the library and determine the publishers,
• recognize and clarify any ambiguities in orders relating to the titles (format or edition) and ambiguities relating to the order (method of supply, the number of copies, receiving location(s), billing location(s), start date, duration, etc.,) and, further,
• notify the library of any requested titles it cannot service.

Publishers in the United States will not activate orders for periodical serials unless they are accompanied by prepayment of the correct subscription amount. Thus, to effect timely placement of an order, an agency must:

• determine the publisher's address,
• identify and resolve any conflict between the publisher's procedures and the library's order,
• determine the subscription rate that applies to the specific title and library,
• issue payment in the appropriate currency,
• generate and dispatch the order and payment, and
• store details of the order and payment for future reference.

These capabilities are also critical for the timely renewal of expiring subscriptions. Renewal has the additional requirement that the agent:

- notify the library of the impending expiration of subscriptions in sufficient time to allow processing of renewals.

An agency that has the structures to support accurate, prompt placement of orders and timely renewals will both limit the need for claims and adjustments and have in place the elements for servicing such claims as arise, being able to:

- identify the library, publisher, title, and order referenced in the claim,
- document the details of the order and payment, and
- generate and dispatch a claim to the publisher.

Many librarians consider that responsive claiming also requires that an agency:

- track responses to claims,
- report the results of claims to the library, and
- initiate further claiming procedures if the publisher is nonresponsive.

These expectations are inappropriate and will cause problems if a library adopts them as its standards for claiming support from an agency. Publishers' responses to claims vary. Some ignore them while others respond by mailing the claimed issue(s) direct to the library. In either case, no agency is in a position to determine whether a response has been made. An agency can only report accurately on the responses it receives directly; it cannot report the results of *all* claims, nor determine whether an appropriate response has been forwarded direct to the library. These aspects of claiming support are more appropriately expressed as requiring that an agency:

- maintain a record of all claims it submits on behalf of the library,
- track the claim responses it receives from publishers,
- report to the library all claims submitted and claim responses received by the agency, and
- upon library notification of claims for which no response has been received, initiate further claiming procedures.

The differences in these two groups of requirements may appear to be minor. But as expressions of library expectations of agency service, they illustrate the importance of libraries clearly delineating their service requirements and expectations.

How can agencies "reduce the expenditure of library resources on . . . order placement, renewal, and fulfillment" in order to become an effective alternative to ordering direct? Standard approaches include: issuing consolidated invoices that can be settled with a single check; providing claiming support, consolidated renewal lists, and management reports; and maintaining accurate title, publisher and pricing data. Agency efficiency is also a factor; an efficient agency can reduce library workloads, an inefficient agency can add to them.

To be effective, an agency must communicate with its clients clearly and unambiguously. The benefits libraries receive from agency services such as consolidated renewal lists and invoices are diminished if the reports use a form of title significantly different from that used in internal library records. Given the many variations in the way different libraries record serials titles, it should be anticipated that there will be some mismatch between the forms of title used by an agency and its clients. [Agency forms of title are shaped by the need to communicate orders to publishers clearly and unambiguously rather than by the access requirements of libraries.]

Certain questions should be asked. What does the agency do to reduce the impact of these variations on libraries? Does it offer a choice in the form of the title used in documentation of a library's account? Does it require that the agency form of title, title number, order number, invoice number, etc. appear on claims and correspondence? If so, what assistance does the agency provide to link the library's records with the agency's form of title or title number? If the agency offers kardex labels printed with its form of title or title number to provide this linkage, are the labels gratis or available only for an additional fee? Are agency listings output in the order in which the library's records are maintained? Can the order and contents of listings be changed without charge to the library? How many copies of such listings does the agency provide as part of its basic service?

An effective agency will not only handle its own procedures efficiently but will also develop services to protect its clients from the impact of publishers' idiosyncracies. For example, library procedures are simplified by receipt of a single consolidated invoice for all subscriptions. Publisher price announcements do not follow a coordinated schedule. As a result, the consolidated invoice issued by an agency is often followed by numerous supplemental invoices covering unexpected price increases, additional billings for special issues, and the like. These supplemental invoices cause additional check processing and paperwork for libraries. An effective agency will seek to limit the impact of additional billings on libraries. Appropriate measures include consolidating additional charges on a single monthly or quarterly adjustment invoice, or absorbing additional billings for an additional service fee.

Similarly, both agencies and libraries know that delivery problems are the norm with certain mass-market titles, and that the publishers of these titles tend to be unresponsive to claims for replacement issues. An astute agent will devise ways of protecting its clients from these problems. The approach may be as informal as going to a newsstand and purchasing thirty copies of the swimsuit issue of *Sports Illustrated*, or a more formal mechanism may be set up. For example, one large U.S. agency maintains a missing issues bank of single issues of popular titles contributed by client libraries and staff. The bank provides replacement for missing issues that are not available from publishers.

Both agencies and libraries need to track bibliographic changes in the serials they handle. Responsive agencies share this information with clients in a format that facilitates its use. A library will find it more convenient to receive customized reports of changes that affect only the titles to which it subscribes than to receive bulletins or reports on changes that affect all the titles that an agency handles. Cost assignment and invoice checking may be facilitated if information on bibliographic changes is also included on agency invoices.

Responsive agents are willing to work with libraries to devise *appropriate* approaches to specific problems or service needs as they arise. In this context the term "appropriate" may mean different things to each party. For a library, an appropriate approach will be one that solves its perceived problem. For some libraries, "appropriate" may also imply that any solution should not incur additional charges. For an agency, "appropriate" will mean "possible," in that the problem and/or solution are in areas the agency can control; "viable," in that the workload and resources the agency expends on the service are minimal, or libraries are agreeable to paying a charge to cover the cost of service provision; and "strategic," in that the investment of resources in this problem at this time is in line with the agency's priorities and will enhance its competitive position in the industry.

For an agency, "appropriate" will mean:

—"possible," in that the problem and/or solution are in areas the agency can control
—"viable," in that the workload and resources the agency expends on the service are minimal or libraries are agreeable to paying a charge to cover the cost of service provision
—and "strategic," in that the investment of resources in this problem at this time is in line with the agency's priorities and will enhance its competitive position in the industry.

INTERNAL AGENCY AUTOMATION

Although the internal automation of subscription agency operations does not constitute a direct service to libraries, it has become an essential prerequisite for the efficient, cost-effective provision of mainstream subscription services. Introduced by the larger agencies in the mid-1960s, automation has streamlined agency operations and significantly increased productivity. By the mid-to late-1970s, internal automation had become essential for agency viability. The lack of automation contributed to the failure of a number of small agencies, and others fell by the wayside under the cost of developing and implementing automated systems. Meanwhile, the larger agencies extended their systems to provide direct automated services to libraries and (to a lesser extent) publishers, a focus which continued through the 1980s.

The impact of internal automation on agency operations is demonstrated by the experience of one large U.S. subscription agency:

> In 1958 we filled 3,500 subscription orders per employee. Now [1976] the average is 5,600. In a nutshell, the computer . . . is performing work which would have required an addition to our staff of 200 people, doubling our manual labor expense, and at the same time has made it possible for us to give better service.[39]

And,

> In 1958, it took twenty-three people . . . to service each 100,000 subscriptions. . . . A conservative translation of the quality and quantity of services of today [1983] into the number of people required to perform these functions in 1958 would mean at least doubling of the 1958 staff. Since 1975, however, productivity gains have been negligible. Today fourteen people are needed for 100,000 service lines. . . .[40]

While no one would challenge this assessment of the contribution of automation to agency efficiency, not all agencies have shared the experience of a levelling out of the productivity gains generated by automation. Smaller agencies using more recent, less expensive, and more flexible automated systems may still achieve productivity gains through automation.

AUTOMATED SERVICES FOR LIBRARIES

The provision of some level of automated service support for libraries is the norm in all but the smallest U.S. subscription agencies. The most common service is electronic communication between agencies and libraries. Implementations range from electronic mail to online access to agencies' internal automated systems with support for electronic messaging, online submission of orders and claims, and access to the vendor's files of title, publisher, and pricing data. Increasingly, agencies are tailoring their services to the automated systems used by libraries, providing machine-readable bibliographic data and invoices that can be loaded into local library systems. Agencies are also developing interfaces to support the direct transfer of data between their systems and local automated library systems and to enable libraries to access vendor services from local library system terminals.

Several agencies offer automated services in areas that are peripheral to traditional agency services: serials check-in and union listing facilities mounted on a central computer system; standalone serials check-in systems based on personal computers; and CD-ROM-based serials directories. The automated products and services offered by the two largest subscription agencies are described in the Appendix. These services are typical of those offered by most agencies serving the North American market.

Serial subscription agencies are not the only source for automated support for serials management in libraries. And, outside of the direct transfer of data—machine-readable invoicing data, ordering, and claiming—it is debatable whether the automated services provided by agencies are necessarily the best way for libraries to meet their needs for automated serials support. However, many librarians regard the provision of a range of automated products and services as a hallmark of a superior agency. For their part, agencies find these services to be a useful marketing tool, encouraging the concentration of a library's serials orders with a single vendor and the long-term commitment of orders to that vendor. The provision of automated services to libraries is often described as a potentially lucrative source of revenue for agencies. However, most observers believe that few agents currently recover the costs of these services from the libraries that use them.

Libraries investigating their options for subscription management should maintain a clear perspective on the role of automation in the provision of subscription services:

> Automation is the byway through which many or all of the service components of a serial vendor are speeded up and made available to many people. . . . When the [library's] object is to obtain serials in a rapid manner, the automation ought to support *this* objective first. This is the basic question the librarian should ask: does this automation help me obtain a serial in a more efficient manner than I do now? If the answer is not a clear "yes," then opting for a serial company with a wide array of automated services that the library will probably not use and will certainly pay for in one way or another, is ill-advised.[41]

Libraries can, and do, benefit from the automated services offered by subscription agencies. However, it should not be assumed that such services are essential to basic subscription management nor that their availability guarantees better handling of a library's subscriptions. If a library needs automated support for serials management, it should explore all options, not just those offered by serial vendors.

SPECIALIZED SERVICES

In addition to basic subscription services and library-oriented automated services, many agencies also provide, or are willing to develop, specialized services to meet the needs of individual libraries or groups of libraries. Issue handling and shipment services are the most common and are typically applied in the supply of non-periodical serials and foreign serials. Materials are shipped from publishers to the agency rather than direct to the library. The agent receives and organizes the material, identifies and claims missing issues, and reships consignments to the library, often by air mail or some other method of accelerated delivery.

Some agencies will perform the full range of check-in and processing activities usually undertaken by library staff: issue check-in, ownership stamping, shelving and routing designation, preparation of management reports, etc. Materials and the associated manual or machine-readable check-in records are forwarded to the library. These services are particularly attractive to libraries with staffing constraints. The National Library of Medicine (NLM) has considerable experience with off-site processing, and has found that:

> . . . studies of the relative times necessary to process directly received items and off-site check-in shipments show that processing dealer check-in items takes less than half the staff time and about one quarter the elapsed time since it lends itself to a team approach. There are concomitant savings in time needed for mail sorting, and in the professional time needed to solve problems associated with the receipt of items not already represented in the NLM file of serial titles, and of course, in the time required for claiming. One interesting benefit is a decrease in time spent processing junk mail.[42]

As with automation, subscription agencies are not the only source for such support. Many other companies and individuals offer contract labor for serials services.

RELATIONS WITH PUBLISHERS

> [Agents] are terribly dependent upon publisher efficiency and goodwill.[43]

> The agent can easily be sabotaged by an inefficient or indifferent publisher.[44]

> Ultimately, the quality of a subscription agent's service depends upon the service [agents] receive from publishers.[45]

Agencies are financially and operationally dependent on publishers. No matter how efficient and responsive an agency, client perceptions of its performance are affected by a variety of publisher practices and procedures, including: the timeliness of order entry and renewal; the accuracy of subscription records; policies on the treatment of claims for missing and damaged issues and refunds for cancelled subscriptions or ceased publications; the timing and frequency of subscription rate changes; procedures for handling orders received immediately following a rate change; and the distribution of information on subscription rates, publication delays, bibliographic changes, and special issues.

Agencies work hard to develop and maintain good working relations with publishers:

[Agents] are terribly dependent upon publisher efficiency and goodwill.[43]

The agent can easily be sabotaged by an inefficient or indifferent publisher.[44]

Ultimately, the quality of a subscription agent's service depends upon the service [agents] receive from publishers.[45]

Not only are library customers wooed by subscription agents; publishers are also courted. . . . The vendors have long had persons at the managerial level whose job is to establish and maintain good working relationships with publishers, both to obtain the best possible financial advantage for agents and to keep agencies informed about activities in the publishing field and specific titles.[46]

Some agencies make substantial investments in developing automated services to facilitate their interaction with publishers: machine-readable orders tailored to the requirements of publisher fulfillment systems, electronic messaging and claim transmittal systems, and online linkages to publishers' bibliographic and information files. Such services have the potential to reduce agency costs, enhance the speed with which transactions are processed, and attract greater discounts from publishers. While agencies are enthusiastic about these services, publishers are the limiting factor in widespread implementation; only the largest have automated systems capable of making use of such services.

Agencies believe that their subscription services benefit publishers as well as libraries:

Agencies now handle such important and time-consuming functions as editing subscription orders for duplication, verifying addresses, and providing new subscription details. Most agencies can supply complete order and payment information on magnetic tape instead of, or in addition to, printed orders. This eliminates the need to keyboard and proofread individual orders, providing significant savings for your fulfillment department.

Acting as clearinghouses, agencies also reduce your overhead costs by answering queries about missing or lost issues. The agency can quickly determine if a customer's order is in good standing and if the publication has, in fact, been issued. Valid claims can then be forwarded with all the information necessary for quick and efficient processing.

The agency takes care of the costly handling procedures usually associated with institutional buyers—issuing and confirming purchase orders, processing state and local vouchers, and converting foreign currency. Further, by consolidating institutional clients into a single purchase order with a common expiration date for all subscriptions, agencies simplify accounting and renewal procedures for both subscribers and publishers.[47]

Two other aspects of subscription agency order handling have particular appeal for publishers of mass-market and consumer magazines. Agency orders are prepaid, eliminating the risk and expense entailed in collecting on "invoice me later" subscriptions to individuals, and library orders have a higher renewal rate than individual subscriptions.

It is difficult to judge the effectiveness of agency publisher relations programs. Each agency has its own approach and each publisher its individual response. Some initiatives bring results. For example, one British publisher who never gave vendors a discount now offers a discount to agencies submitting orders on magnetic tape. However, continuing problems in the supply of titles handled by fulfillment centers reinforce the impression that neither libraries nor subscription agencies are of importance to many mass-market publishers.

Publishers have been relatively silent on their views of agencies. Agencies (and libraries) appear to be little more than thorns in the side of some publishers, but they are of great significance to others, providing a steady stream of orders and renewals which the publishers would be hard pressed to replace through other arrangements. Eighty percent of subscriptions to the *Library Journal* are placed through agencies.

In the scholarly publishing field, some societies derive as much as 60 to 70 percent of their total operating income from nonmember subscriptions. One society receives 94 percent of its subscription orders from agencies, and it is not unusual for agencies to provide more than 80 percent of a publisher's total subscriptions.[48] In such situations, it is easy to assume that agencies are in a position to exercise considerable influence on publishers. This is not the case. Despite their significance as a source of orders for societal publishers, agencies rarely receive discounts from societies and associations.

The whole concept of publishers providing discounts to agencies is neither universally accepted, not guaranteed for the future by those publishers that currently recognize it.

The question of agency clout with publishers arises in a variety of situations. Agency representatives sometimes cite their special relationship with publishers as a direct benefit accruing to libraries that use subscription agency services. Sometimes agencies broaden this line of reasoning by presenting themselves as library advocates, willing and able to represent library interests and viewpoints to the publishing community. Many librarians find it difficult to reconcile this view of the agency-publisher relationship with the apparent inability of agencies to persuade publishers to change practices that have a negative impact on library operations such as curtailing the flood of publisher renewal notices that continues to descend on libraries that use agencies to handle their subscriptions. Such confusion is understandable. In the authors' opinion, the reality is that

> [T]he myth persists that periodical agencies can exercise some control over publisher business practices and pricing policies simply because of the large volume of orders funnelled through the agencies by libraries. There is generally a cooperative spirit that moves publishers and subscription agencies to cooperate for the purpose of reducing or containing service costs, but neither attempts to tell the other how to operate its business.[49]

To varying degrees, agencies also view publishers as a market capable of generating real income in addition to notional receipts in the form of discounts and improved service. At the simplest level, publishers can be a healthy source of advertising income for agencies' catalogs. Dedicated pursuit of this opportunity can make an agency's annual catalog a profit center rather than an expense. In more sophisticated (but possibly less profitable) applications, some agencies offer publishers electronic advertising opportunities, including their publications in online files accessed by libraries. Other agencies sell shelf space in their exhibits at library conventions, enabling publishers to display their titles without the expense of mounting individual booths.

CATEGORIZING SUBSCRIPTION AGENCIES

Subscription agencies can be categorized in many ways. Librarians and agents usually distinguish among agencies on the basis of size, location, and/or specialization. Publishers approach agencies from a different perspective, distinguishing between agencies that serve libraries and other institutions and *field* agencies which offer support for a more limited range of titles and usually target their services to individual subscribers rather than institutions.

Size: Agency size has implications for costs, the range of services supported, and service style. Larger agencies have higher overheads but provide a wider range of services. Smaller agencies may provide more personalized service with lower overheads and lower costs. Many commentators advise that:

> Small to medium-sized libraries, those requiring few services other than placing of orders and attending to claims, should deal with a small agent. Medium-sized to large libraries, depending again upon list size and service requirements, should select one of the medium-sized to larger agents.[50]

Numerous measures can be used to determine the size of a subscription agency: annual revenues, number of orders processed, number of titles for which orders are maintained, number of clients, etc. Most subscription agencies are privately held and do not reveal such data. Whatever the measures or guesstimates used, size is relative. Boss and McQueen surveyed thirteen U.S. subscription agencies in 1989.[51] Ten of the agencies provided revenue figures, four reporting annual revenues of less than $5 million, one revenues between $5 and $15 million, two between $15 and $30 million, and one between $60 and $150 million. Two agencies reported more than $250 million in annual revenues. Thus, in the U.S., an agency with annual revenues of less than $5 million can be considered small and one with more than $250 million very large. What of those between $5 million and $250 million? Leaving aside the industry giants, an agency with revenues approaching $100 million would have to be considered large.

Location: It is common to distinguish among subscription agencies based on location, the most usual breakdown being between domestic and foreign agencies, with foreign agencies being further subdivided by regional or language orientation. In North America, the distinction between domestic and foreign agencies is somewhat blurred. Canadian and U.S. agencies follow similar practices, removing one of the grounds for the distinction; the larger agencies are international in their coverage of mainstream publications; and the size of the market is such that a number of European agencies find it sufficiently attractive to modify their practices and procedures to meet local service expectations. The majority of North American libraries find that a U.S. or Canadian agency can adequately service their serials acquisition needs. Those with large numbers of European titles may find it advantageous to investigate the services and pricing of European agencies. Generally, it is only libraries with exotic interests that need to consider agencies that are foreign in both their location and procedures.

There is considerable uniformity in the services, procedures, and capabilities of North American agencies and major European agencies that target the North American market; other foreign agents are more varied. Such variations present both opportunities and risks. North American agents have traditionally focussed on the supply of current periodical serials. While "willing to handle monographic series, books-in-part, government documents, and retrospective orders [back issues], . . . their expertise in doing so varies."[52] As a result many U.S. libraries place their orders for such materials with book jobbers rather than subscription agencies. In North America, "*subscription* agency" is a meaningful term: agencies are best able to handle materials available on subscription. In contrast, many European agencies have strong links to the book trade and a tradition of supplying back issues as well as current subscriptions. A European agent may be able to provide better services in these areas than a U.S. agency.

When dealing with any agency, but especially foreign agencies, (even European agencies attuned to the North American market), a library must take care to state and confirm what are usually unstated assumptions about subscription agency services and procedures. For instance, most U.S. agencies treat periodical serials on an annual renewal basis, i.e., at the end of a subscription period, an order lapses unless it is actively renewed. Agencies issue renewal lists to facilitate subscription review and renewal. Many libraries rely on these lists to trigger related internal procedures such as weeding and cost allocation. In contrast, many suppliers and publishers in continental Europe handle subscriptions on a "'til forbid" basis, automatically renewing all current subscriptions until a subscriber specifically requests cancellation.[53] Many European publishers do not require advance payment to ensure continued supply; rather they continue the supply of material and issue invoices as appropriate. New subscription prices may not be announced in advance, and price changes may not be advised until they are in effect. These procedures eliminate the need for formal advance renewal action, so agencies that specialize in the supply of European serials from countries other than Britain may not be in the habit of providing renewal lists to their library clients. This can pose problems for libraries that rely on the receipt of renewal lists to activate internal procedures. Most foreign agencies can generate renewal lists, but a library must remember to request this service.

Vendors may also differ in their procedures for calculating and presenting service charges:

Foreign vendors have customarily included an unspecified service charge in the price for each periodical title, but they now appear to be turning to the American practice of adding a percentage to the total of the list prices.[54]

While this illustrates another area in which the practices of non-domestic vendors vary from standard local practice, it is interesting to note that recent developments appear to be modifying the local standard. As a result of the debate on price increases for commercial STM publications, at least one publisher has required that its publications appear on agency invoices showing zero service charge, in recognition of the discounts it advances to agencies. In adjusting their systems to comply with this requirement, some U.S. agencies have developed the ability to offer invoices that break out service charges item by item, rather than presenting them as a separate line applying to the invoice as a whole.

Forewarned to confirm expectations and clearly state their needs, most libraries have little difficulty accommodating the different practices of major North American and European agencies. It can be more challenging to deal with agencies located in other parts of the world.

The regional focus of an agency is an important and potentially frustrating concern for library managers with collections rich in foreign titles. Crossing any national boundary entails currency and communication problems. These appear to be least troublesome in relation to English-language publications and those from Western Europe. Real difficulties arise for libraries requiring publications from Third World countries and other areas subject to political and economic instability. It is not only difficult to find reliable subscription agency coverage for such areas, but whatever service is available is fragmented and requires libraries to deal with multiple, small vendors rather than several large suppliers.

Specialty Agencies: Some agencies target specific sectors of the library market, tailoring their services to the needs of school libraries, medical and hospital libraries, public libraries, or special libraries. While specialization does not necessarily guarantee superior service or pricing, librarians in market sectors served by specialist agents should investigate their services along with those of more generalist agencies. Some specialist vendors offer service for all types of materials, monographs, and serials. This can be advantageous for libraries with serials collections that include significant numbers of non-periodical serials.

Field Agencies: Library subscription agents or "catalog" agents as they are known to publishers, should not be confused with "field" agents. Field agents handle a limited number of popular, mass-circulation specialty titles, in business, news, and fashion, and sell subscriptions at discounts ranging from 30 to 50 percent below list price. Field agents often specialize in such titles, or they may be members of schools, churches, or other organizations involved in fund raising. They market their titles through a combination of direct mail, telemarketing, and door to door sales.

Field agents focus on sales to individuals, the type of subscriber who most interests the publishers of mass circulation titles that rely on advertising income rather than income from subscriptions. The publishers of these titles have a strong interest in developing and maintaining a large subscriber base to attract advertising. Thus, they see deep price discounting as a worthwhile expenditure for increased circulation figures. The discounts to field agencies can be as high as 80 to 90 percent, readily enabling them to cover costs while still offering subscriptions at an attractive discount.

Unlike catalog agencies which prepay orders to publishers and bill the library for this expenditure, field agents usually require payment at the time the order is lodged with the agent. Some field agencies offer Payment During Service (PDS) options, or time-payment plans. Orders placed with field agents are subject to a cooling down period that allows purchasers of unsolicited goods and services to cancel orders without penalty within a specific timeframe.

Field agencies generally handle only order placement and problem resolution; they may forward claims to publishers but do not provide auxiliary services such as the tracking of bibliographic changes and report generation. Field agents can be an attractive source of minimum cost subscriptions for libraries that can accommodate orders addressed to individuals.

Sales representatives who market titles from a single publisher are also sometimes referred to as field agents. Publishers that maintain field sales representatives tend to offer specialized titles to a specialized clientele—high-cost, frequently updated serials services in the fields of law, business, and finance—and to focus on sales volume and servicing clients' special needs rather than on discounting.

3 THE SUBSCRIPTION AGENCY BUSINESS

The subscription agency business is highly competitive with relatively low percentage profit margins. An efficient, well-managed agency can return a pre-tax profit of from half of one percent to five percent of annual sales. The business has the potential for steady returns.

Serials subscription agencies are in the *service* business. Unlike most other vendors serving libraries, subscription agencies neither produce nor distribute commodities. Their sole purpose is to provide services to facilitate the acquisition of serials by libraries. It is notoriously difficult to define and evaluate the quality of services, and it can be tempting to assume that the largest agencies provide the best service. The temptation should be resisted since there is no compelling evidence of a lasting relationship between vendor size and library perceptions of service quality. Subscription agencies are in the service *business*. No matter how appropriate and responsive the service an agency offers, it will not survive, let alone succeed, unless it can strike a profitable balance between the cost of providing service and the price the market is prepared to pay for those services.

This chapter examines the business aspects of subscription agency operations: the market, the cost of servicing that market, and the sources of revenue available to cover costs and profit requirements. Although the environment is common to all agencies, individual agencies differ in how they operate within that environment. Different agencies have different business styles and follow different practices. An approach that is standard in one agency may be unheard of in another. And agency cultures and practices change over time. Such changes may be triggered by the external environment. For example, the focus of library needs and sensitivities may shift, the marketing stances of competing vendors may alter, or publisher policies may change. Internal changes may include changes in the ownership or management of an agency.

An appreciation of the business aspects of subscription agency operations is essential for librarians responsible for serials acquisition. It a prerequisite for informed decisions on whether to use an agency and which agency or agencies to use. Moreover, it can be invaluable both in negotiating initial service and pricing packages and in monitoring service provision.

THE MARKETPLACE

Subscription agents consider the library market for subscription service mature. Their growth opportunities are limited to capturing accounts from other agents, developing and selling new services to libraries, nurturing nontraditional markets (among publishers, for instance), and the natural growth in revenues attendant upon the increasing number of serials and rising serial prices. Most agents consider the library market to be conservative, reluctant to change suppliers, and demanding in its service expectations.

Although each library has its own identity, user base, and collections, libraries of the same type have similar subscription service needs. Agencies typically divide the market into the following segments:

• College, university and research libraries,
• Public libraries,
• School libraries,
• Medical and health science libraries,
• Law libraries,
• Government libraries, and
• Corporate and other institutional libraries.

Each group of libraries purchases different types of serials. Academic and research libraries and medical libraries typically subscribe to significant numbers of STM publications. Such materials are rarely found in school libraries and smaller public libraries, which have collections with a high proportion of general and specialist consumer titles. Law and medical library subscriptions are skewed towards the output of specialist publishers, and corporate library lists generally include numerous weekly and newsletter services. These differences are reflected in the average prices of the serials purchased by each market segment. For 1988 subscriptions, the average list prices by market segment for orders handled by one large U.S. agency were:[55]

College and university	$117.75
High schools	$ 32.94
Primary schools	$ 32.89
Public libraries	$ 54.78
Business libraries	$157.70
Hospital libraries	$137.86
Government libraries	$146.40

Different market segments have different service needs. Corporate libraries that bill back subscriptions to specific departments or projects may require special invoicing and accounting procedures; government libraries generally require special billing and renewal procedures; academic and research libraries frequently require machine-readable bibliographic and invoicing data; and school libraries and smaller college libraries may be unable to process invoices and renewal lists during the summer break.

MARGINS

Agents address costs and pricing from a perspective that differs from that of libraries. The prices publishers charge agencies are an important consideration in agency operations. The amount of money the agency must forward to a publisher to effect a subscription is known as the *publisher's price* or *remittance amount*. This will be the same as the *published price*, *retail price*, or *list price*— the publisher's advertised price—if a publisher does not offer a discount to agencies. When a publisher grants a discount to agencies, the remittance amount will be lower than the list price.

Agencies operate on *margins*, the difference between the remittance price forwarded to publishers and the total price for subscriptions and services charged to libraries. Most agencies use a notional minimum margin when pricing their services, seeking to recover the remittance amount plus a specified percentage or dollar amount on each account. The size of the margin will vary from agency to agency, and within an agency it may vary from market sector to market sector.

An agency may have different margin objectives for different market sectors. Some markets are more costly to service than others. Special libraries frequently make substantial changes in their subscription lists and may require extremely fast and responsive service for the placement of new orders. They also tend to be demanding in the claiming support they expect from an agent. Their demands on an agency's customer service personnel are greater than are those of other types of libraries. On the other hand, libraries with very large accounts often expect regular and frequent visits from their local sales representative and agency managers. Academic and research libraries may require more customized development of automated support services—special formatting of machine-readable invoicing data to save the effort of re-keying the data into local automated systems, custom interfaces between local library systems and agency systems to support the transmission of orders and claims, etc. If an agency does not levy separate charges for such development, it will be more expensive to service the automation requirements of this sector than those of other markets. Agencies do not necessarily establish margin requirements that reflect the costs of serving different market segments; that is but one possible approach.

The actions of competing agencies can also be influential. An agency attempting to break into a market in which it does not have a significant presence may use pricing to penetrate the market. If the newcomer has lower costs or lower margin objectives than the agencies already serving the market, the established agencies may have to lower their prices (and thus their margins) to retain accounts.

Margin objectives are set to cover all agency costs plus profit requirements. They may be expressed as a dollar amount—an average of $10 an invoice line, for example—or as a percentage of either the remittance price or list price for a library's total order. One agency may try to achieve its margin objectives on every invoice line or every account, another may be prepared to "lose on the swings and gain on the roundabout," seeking to achieve a specified average margin on all orders and, within that objective, adjusting pricing to meet individual client needs and concerns. Two libraries using the same agency to service identical lists of titles may pay significantly different prices for the use of the same services if the vendor's awareness of one library's high sensitivity to price results in it making a lower bid than it advances to a library less concerned about cost.

If generous publisher discounts or lower percentage discounts but a high retail price for the titles in a specific library's list result in remittance prices significantly lower than the list prices, an agency may still achieve its margin objectives by offering the titles at a discount—a price lower than the published or list price—or at the list price with no service charge.

The cost that a library manager identifies as a service charge or handling fee—the amount of an invoice over and above the total of list prices for the items on an invoice—is, in most cases, only part of an agency's margin. The other part of the margin—the difference between the remittance price and the list price—is usually invisible to customers and has, until recently, been considered a closely guarded secret in most agencies.[56]

The veil of secrecy that has surrounded remittance prices and agency margins may be lifting. In the face of protests about serials price inflation, some publishers are publicizing the discounts they provide to agents. They present the discounts as a direct benefit to libraries because the discounts subsidize agency costs that would otherwise be borne by libraries. Some publishers are requiring that agencies emphasize this contribution by handling discounted titles at the standard subscription price without any additional service charge. Such developments do not require that agencies reveal the extent of the discounts they receive and thus the full amount of their margins. However, it can be expected that libraries will become more aware of publisher discounts and agency service charges.

Despite price increases and budget erosion, library concern about the cost of agency services is far from universal. For those libraries for which cost is a major consideration, the bottom line is the total amount billed by an agency—the cost of individual subscriptions, plus any service charge, plus any charges for additional products or services which the agency bills separately. The bottom line on individual accounts matters more to cost-sensitive libraries than to an agency. While most agencies seek to recover a specific margin on each account, they are prepared to accept lower margins on cost-sensitive accounts and to make up the difference by levying higher charges on the accounts of libraries that are less cost conscious.

An agency's room for negotiation depends on the size of its margin. This varies with the discounts the agency receives from publishers, the cost of agency operations, the agency's profit objectives, and the cost sensitivity of its market—the extent of the service charges customers are prepared to pay.

AGENCY COSTS

In some ways, agencies have the same needs as libraries. Agencies must fund space, utilities, furniture and equipment, supplies, and communications, such as mail, phone, fax, and data transmission. They also need literate, knowledgeable staff and, in clerical operations, personnel with a flair for detail. Like libraries, agencies must provide competitive wages and benefits. Agencies incur expenses for travel and meetings, advertising, sales and marketing, public relations, and the production of catalogs, brochures, stationary, and forms. They also face substantial costs for automation, and for finance.

All agencies incur the same types of costs. What concerns a library is the efficiency with which an agency balances its costs. All other things being equal, including the margins of profit sought by different agencies, an agency with lower costs will be able to service a library's account for a lower price than an agency with higher costs. The relationship between individual cost factors is complex. An agency located in an area with low labor costs may be able to provide service at a lower cost than one located in an area of high labor costs. On the other hand, an agency in an area with high labor charges may reduce its dependence on clerical support by developing an automated system that enables it to process orders with a minimum of human intervention.

AUTOMATION

Reference has been made to the pivotal role of automation in agency operations. Agency automation is expensive. Most librarians are familiar with the costs associated with multi-function, integrated automated library systems. Subscription agency systems can be equally complex and are more expensive because of the need for custom development. Since the introduction of the first commercially viable turnkey automated system for libraries in 1974, it has become increasingly rare for libraries to develop their own in-house automated systems. The majority of libraries that have automated have used turnkey automated systems or supported software packages developed for libraries or for broader applications. The costs of developing and maintaining the software are assumed by a vendor, and each client bears only a portion of these costs. This route is not available to subscription agencies, which constitute a small and highly specialized group, in which competitive concerns would make shared software an unthinkable proposition. Subscription agency automation thus entails de novo design, programming, development and maintenance, and the accompanying need for specialist programming staff.

It is interesting to speculate on the comparative costs and benefits of automation for the subscription agencies that pioneered the automation of agency operations and those that automated later. The pioneers have enjoyed cost savings for a longer period, presumably maximizing their competitive advantage. On the other hand, their systems were developed on expensive mainframe hardware and were designed to support internal operations with no thought of the revenue and service potential of providing automated services for libraries. The companies that automated early have adapted their systems to meet these library opportunities but presumably at greater cost than their competitors with less expensive and more flexible hardware and software.

The sophistication and flexibility of an agency's internal system are important factors in determining the cost of agency operations, the range of services supported, and the ease with which new services can be developed. All can have a significant impact on agency viability. It is difficult for outsiders to assess these aspects of agency operations, and it is just as difficult for the personnel associated with one agency to assess the systems and efficiency of another agency. Neither hardware configuration nor software capabilities are reliable indicators of system efficiency, flexibility, or maintenance and enhancement costs. Experience can be an advantage not because of the age of the system but because of the design of the system, which comprehends the common and exceptional conditions that may arise in subscription management.

THE COST OF MONEY

Subscription agencies face a significant cost that is outside the realm of most library budgeting and cost allocation procedures: the cost of money. This also represents a major risk factor in agency operations.

Few U.S. publishers will accept a subscription order unless it is accompanied by payment. It is standard practice for subscription agencies to forward payment with the order, even if the library has not yet paid the agency's invoice. Herein lies both the cost and the risk. With respect to cost, the agency has to find the cash to pay the publishers. If the money is borrowed from an external source, the agency will incur finance charges until the loan is repaid by revenues from its library clients. If the agency finances the transaction from its internal resources, similar costs are incurred in the loss of interest income from the funds tied up in floating payments to publishers.

The risk is also obvious. Agencies pay publishers in the expectation that libraries will honor their orders and pay agency invoices within the agreed time frame, usually thirty days from receipt. The risk is qualified. Libraries in developed countries usually meet their commitments . . . eventually; the risk lies in the timing of payments. It is not unusual for libraries to delay invoice settlement for sixty to ninety days. If an agency has calculated its costs on the basis of payment within thirty days, it will lose money on these accounts. Some agencies seek to recover such losses by levying late payment charges of up to 1.5 percent per month on outstanding invoices. But this option is not always available; some libraries are prohibited from paying such charges by legislation or regulation. When dealing with libraries in countries subject to political or economic instability, most agencies require payment before placing orders.

Payments to publishers are significant even for a small agency. Payments by an agency with annual revenues of $15 million can amount to $13.5 million. A large agency with revenues of $300 million can expect to forward $270 million to publishers each year. It is not difficult to see the impact of even a thirty day lag between payment to publishers and receipt of money from a library. For an agency paying $100 million a year to publishers and borrowing at 10 percent per annum, an average delay of thirty days on payments from libraries would cost in excess of $833,000 in interest.

However, the cost of money can also benefit an agency. Astute management of the timing of invoice production and the forwarding of payments to publishers can provide an agency with a significant pool of cash for short-term investment, returning the same ten percent as income rather than as a cost. Skilled cash management can be a major factor in the success of a subscription agency. As one agency president has said of cash management in a high volume agency:

> You can get into $100 million in foreign payments in a day. You can make $500 in a day in waiting for publishers to cash checks.[57]

In North America, most libraries place their subscriptions on a calendar year basis. To sustain this schedule, publishers must receive renewal notification and payment before the end of the year. Scheduling varies from publisher to publisher, but most expect to have orders and payment in hand by early November. Given publishers' procedures and libraries' concerns to ensure continuity in receipt of serials, it would clearly be unwise for an agency (or a library that orders direct from publishers) to delay renewal notification and payment until the eleventh hour. The usual pattern is for agencies to distribute renewal lists in June and July and to issue invoices as soon as the renewal lists are returned. The peak months for invoicing are July through October.

Although many librarians criticize agents for issuing invoices months in advance of subscription expiration dates, others feel that they do not issue them early enough:

... the fiscal year begins on October 1, and the serials department has had to make special arrangements to receive at least some agency invoices by late August or early September. The library wants to pay the renewals before the end of the fiscal year in order to avoid losing January and February issues due to the renewal of the subscription not being entered in time. The University business office is flooded with invoices from other University offices at the beginning of the fiscal year and may fall as much as six weeks behind in making payments during the October-November period, a period crucial to renewals for the new calendar year. Despite the supposed avariciousness of agencies, the library has a hard time convincing agencies to invoice as early as August because it is in the interests of the agencies to run all their renewal invoices in a batch, if possible, and to avoid as far as possible the bookkeeping associated with price adjustments.[58]

Many school libraries also require a non-standard invoicing cycle. They tend to start subscriptions in September with the new school year. To take account of this pattern, each step in the renewal-invoicing-order-payment cycle for school libraries is stepped back by at least four months. The step-back is at least four months, because the summer vacation period places many school librarians out of reach from June through September, complicating finalization of renewals and payment of invoices during these months.

The production of an invoice serves as the agent's signal to create an order to be forwarded to the publisher *with payment*. Despite the standard "invoice payable within thirty days" caveat, payments from libraries tend to trickle in from September into the new year. Agencies have some discretion in the timing of order placement and payment; money received from a library at the beginning of September might not be sent to the publisher until mid-November, for instance. In some cases, the interests of subscription continuity can require that an agency hold renewals and payments for some time—for example, when there is a possibility that premature dispatch to the publisher would result in early renewal of a subscription and consequent unintended duplication. An agency may also withhold renewals and payments when a publisher is seriously behind in its production schedule. On the other hand, prepayment of publishers is such an accepted part of agency services that a library that fails to pay its invoice until January is unlikely to accept its late payment as an excuse for late subscription renewals and consequent missing issues.

A library that has the ability to pay invoices promptly or even in advance of the normal cycle can share in the investment benefits:

> . . . early invoicing of subscription renewals [means that the] . . . agent receives the library's money several months before it must be paid to the publishers. The funds are invested and bring additional revenue to the agent. Often the library receives a small share of the interest on the agent's investment, which can be applied to renewal charges or other payments to the vendor. Because most libraries are not able to invest materials funds themselves, this means of reducing costs is attractive.[59]

Some agencies voluntarily reward libraries for early payment by varying their handling charges according to the month in which payment is made. The earlier the payment, the lower the service charge. If a library has the ability to pay its invoice well before the end of the subscription year and its agent does not offer recognition of the value of such an advance payment, the serials manager should negotiate for a reduction in the service charge or other appropriate recompense.

While it would be foolhardy to delay payment to publishers to the point where it disrupts the continual supply of serials, there is room for maneuver. Because their systems are geared for the issuance of renewal lists, invoices, and orders and checks to publishers, subscription agents have greater flexibility and support for fine tuning the timing of payments to publishers than is available to most libraries. An agency familiar with the procedures of the publishers to which the agency makes large payments will have a feel for the impact of the timing of renewal orders and payments on the fulfillment procedures of the individual publishers. For instance, it may be possible to delay payments to publishers of monthly journals longer than for weekly publications without disrupting supply. Similarly there may be room for longer delays in the renewal of subscriptions to quarterly journals which distribute their first issue in March than for quarterlies that publish their first issues in January. It can be very attractive to hold back $500,000 worth of prepaid orders for a week or two and thus earn or avoid interest on that money.

In 1989, one large U.S. agency formalized what had previously been a selective practice in delaying payments to publishers. The agency forwarded its renewal orders in mid-November accompanied by checks postdated for December 22 (the last business day before the holiday period). The move brought unfavorable reactions from both librarians and publishers. Librarians expressed concern about disruption in serials supply and the effect of late payment on publishers' discounting policies; publishers pointed to increased costs relating to the bulking of order processing and the loss of revenues attendant upon delayed payment. Several publishers indicated that they would consider prorating agency discounts on the basis of the timing of order renewals and payments—an approach similar to the one agencies use in providing incentives for libraries to prepay invoices.[60]

The submission of orders and renewals to publishers in machine-readable form has the potential to increase the leeway available to agencies, narrowing the delay between publishers' receipt of orders and the entry of the data into their fulfillment systems. For publishers, the electronic submission of renewals has both advantages and disadvantages:

> Receiving renewals on magnetic tape is beneficial to publishers who have this capability. Magnetic tape allows faster updating of the subscription records and reduces data entry errors at the publisher's office . . . Magnetic tape orders need to be received by the first part of November, as do paper orders, in case there are problems with the tape.[61]

> The use of tape transfer fell short of our expectations. These expectations . . . centered around earlier receipt of orders and payments, as well as savings in clerical and processing effort. We did not receive the anticipated efficiencies, at least not to the extent we hoped. More importantly, we experienced no improvement in the timing of subscription renewals. On the contrary, there appeared to be a slowing down in the flow, as illustrated by the distribution of dollars . . .[62]

> In . . . tape transfer, one obvious factor affecting the timeliness of orders and payments is the date of transmission. With paper transmission, the flow of orders was more or less continuous on a week-by-week basis. Weekly transfers by tape have been considered impractical, with the result that there are now month-long intervals between receipt of orders. Depending on when the tapes are run, this means that some orders are received up to three weeks later than they would be under the more continuous transfer of paper.[63]

When available, electronic fund transfers can be timed to the minute, offering agencies additional control over the timing of payments to publishers.

REVENUE SOURCES

Service charges are the most obvious source of subscription agency revenues. Of equal importance, but less obvious, are the notional revenues that accrue from publisher discounts. Agencies also derive subsidiary income from other sources including: sale of advertising space in agency catalogs and online information systems; conference display services; automated products and services for libraries and publishers; and revenues generated from cash management. Sources of miscellaneous income and the significance of its contribution to revenues vary from agency to agency.

As privately held corporations, subscription agencies do not reveal revenue figures. However, the authors' informed estimate is that the largest agencies still derive at least half of their revenues from publisher discounts. Service charges are rapidly assuming equal importance. Miscellaneous income accounts for only a small proportion of overall revenues—probably from half of one percent to five percent of total sales.

PUBLISHER DISCOUNTS

Although not all publishers offer discounts, subscription agencies derive substantial revenues from those who do. When discounts are available, agencies receive remittance prices that are lower than the published prices for subscriptions placed direct with no agency intervention. Agencies bill their clients the standard subscription price but pay publishers the discount price. Agency revenues accrue from the differential between the list price and the remittance or discount price. Until the 1960s, publisher discounts were the only significant source of agency revenues.

Agents tend to be closemouthed about discounts; they rarely reveal details about the levels of discounts they receive from specific publishers, titles, or market segments. Publishers have also had little to say on the subject. In the current climate of library concern over increases in serials prices, some publishers have become more vocal about their discounts to agencies, presenting them as a contribution to cost containment in libraries.

Publishers' discounting practices vary. Some publishers do not offer discounts for orders received from agents, other publishers offer varying discounts, and publishers may negotiate different levels of discount with different agents. [In the United States, a publisher who offers discounts to agents is required by law to provide the same level of discount to all agencies that provide the publisher with the same level of service. This does not preclude the publisher offering different levels of discount for different levels of service—additional discounts for additional services such as the provision of orders in machine-readable form, for example. Foreign publishers are not subject to these regulations. They are free to establish different discounting policies for different agencies, even if the agencies provide identical services.]

Many mass market magazine publishers give significant percentage discounts, and publishers frequently discount prices for foreign orders received through subscription agents. Some publishers offer higher discounts for new orders than for renewals. Some international publishers provide significantly higher discounts to European agents than to North American companies. Others offer a standard trade discount but will negotiate additional trade discounts with larger trade customers who negotiate the size and scheduling of their orders in advance, submit orders in machine-readable form, and undertake special promotions to increase publisher sales. Some research library systems that buy hundreds of thousands of dollars worth of publications from foreign publishers are beginning to negotiate with the publishers for discounts for quantity orders placed direct. As a rule, scholarly publishers—associations and university presses—do not offer discounts to agencies.

Why do some publishers provide discounts while others do not? Part of the explanation can be found in the focus of the publisher. Publishers of mass circulation titles have traditionally been more interested in circulation figures than subscription revenues and are prepared to advance relatively handsome discounts to agencies for the delivery of a large and stable circulation base. Those publishers that rely on subscriptions as their major source of revenue are less interested in reducing their income by offering discounts to agencies. However, some will provide a small discount in recognition of the savings they realize from agency services such as order clarification and consolidation and interfacing with foreign clients. There are no hard and fast rules and few reliable patterns.

Publisher discounts are by no means guaranteed. Their availability and size have been declining since the early 1960s. Describing this decline, Frank Clasquin observed in 1976 that "[a]gency revenue from publishers has narrowed by 33 percent in the last 12 years, i.e., the margin expressed as a percentage of the published rate has been reduced."[64] However during the late 1980s, the impact of the decline in discount percentages for certain categories of serials—particularly titles from commercial publishers—was offset by increases in the price of journals. In some instances, prices increased sufficiently to enable agencies to service these titles at no service charge, despite stable percentage discounts from publishers.

Most agencies track the contribution of publisher discounts by market segment. The authors' informed estimates suggest that in 1989 the average discounts agencies received for the titles purchased by academic, business, and government libraries was 5 to 6 percent of list price. Their estimates for other market segments are: 6 to 7 percent for medical library lists, 9 to 10 percent for public libraries, and 15 to 16 percent for school libraries.

Publishers of certain mass market titles advance large discounts to field agencies that focus on selling magazines to individual subscribers. The discounts are significantly higher than those offered to serials subscription agencies that focus on institutional orders. For publishers that rely on revenue generated from advertising, a subscriber base of the names of individuals is a more valuable commodity than a subscriber list of institutional names. Several serials subscription agencies operate small field agencies as associated enterprises or channel orders for named individuals through external field agencies. These sources often provide substantially higher discounts for subscriptions mailed to individuals and those for waiting rooms or reception areas than are available for orders placed through standard subscription agency channels.

SERVICE CHARGES

Subscription agencies save libraries money. In many transactions, agency costs exceed revenues from publisher discounts. The shortfall is made up by the service fees agencies levy for handling a library's account:

> The cost of the agent's service to place orders and insure regular receipt of journals currently varies from 10 to 12% of the published price. When no clearance margin [discount] is allowed by the publishers or it is less than this amount, the agent adds a service charge. . . . The charge for service . . . compensate[s] the agency for the difference between the total service and operating costs plus return on investment and the clearance margin.[65]

As with publisher discounts there are no hard and fast rules. Costs vary from agency to agency, and agencies are free to set service charges at any levels they please. The lower limit is determined by an agency's need to stay in business, the upper limit by the cost sensitivity of libraries and the service charges of competing agencies. Within these limits, there is considerable room for negotiation by libraries that are concerned about costs.

> The percentage of the charge varies according to the mix of titles on the library's list, the agent's overhead, and how badly the agent wants the library's business.[66]

Just as an agency can choose to levy service charges on any or all transactions, it can also choose to offer discounts. As with service fees, an agency's policy on discounts will be affected by the practices of competing agencies and the expectations of the market being served. For instance, most school libraries and small and medium sized public libraries expect to receive subscription agency service at no service fee and often at a slight discount. On the other hand, service charges are the norm in academic libraries. Although their collections frequently include the same mass market titles that form the bulk of school and public library lists, academic libraries rarely receive discounts or gratis service on these titles unless they segment their lists and actively pursue these opportunities.

Librarians' Attitudes to Service Charges: When service charges were first introduced, many librarians were perturbed, having chosen to use an agency because:

> . . . the agent offered a discount, thereby lowering costs.[67]

Subscription agencies had:

> . . . made the understandable error of convincing the librarian that the agent was quite literally being paid for his order work by the publisher. And, in the confusion, not many librarians stopped to consider that the agent was, indeed, marking up the price of the periodical or, if you will, adding a service charge. The service charge never came to the surface because a title for which the library would have to pay the publisher $10 was sold to the library by the agent for $9. The agent did not bother to say that the publisher had given him the title for $8, and the extra dollar was his service charge or gross markup.[68]

Consequently,

> The introduction of the service charge in the late 1960s and early 1970s . . . [made it appear] that librarians were suddenly being charged for service that was formerly free.[69]

For many, unease was increased by comparisons between subscription agents and monograph vendors. Book vendors provide acquisition services similar to those that subscription agents offer for serials. In comparison with serials vendors, monograph jobbers routinely handle the materials they sell, warehousing, packing, and shipping the items to libraries. Despite these added service levels, most book vendors do not charge a service fee and many offer discounts. Monograph and serials publishers follow different discounting practices. Book publishers typically offer discounts of between 10 and 46 percent of list price, enabling jobbers to meet their costs and still pass on part of the discount to libraries.[70]

The norms changed during the 1970s and 1980s. Except in school and public libraries, most librarians came to recognize that a library that wishes to avail itself of agency support for serials acquisitions will incur service charges on at least part of its account. However, not all practitioners recognize that a library can play an active role in determining the extent of these fees.

To be effective participants in service fee assessment and negotiation, library managers need more than a general awareness of agency costs, revenue sources, and margins. They must know how service charges are determined and the extent of the charges. In addition, they must clarify what services are covered by the service fee and identify any services that are subject to additional charges, and compare the practices of different agencies and the experiences of other libraries. These topics are addressed in the following sections.

How Much is Your Service Fee? Many librarians are not aware of the extent of the service fees levied on their accounts. Service fee evaluation and assessment require an accurate determination of the fees being charged.

Agents figure their margins on the difference between the remittance price they forward to publishers to effect an order and the total charges billed to a customer. Remittance prices are usually treated as confidential; they do not play a part in discussions of service fees between libraries and vendors. In these discussions, service fees are generally defined as the difference between the total of published list prices for the titles to which a library subscribes and the amount the library pays for standard subscription service. Agencies differ in how they describe and present service charges. For comparative purposes, services fees are generally expressed as a percentage of the list price of the subscriptions covered by the charge. If the annual subscription cost for a library's list is $10,000, and its agency invoice is for $10,750, the service fee on the account is 7.5 percent.

It may not be easy to determine the service charge levied on a library's account. Agency management procedures differ from those of libraries. Agency accounting systems track margins and do not necessarily provide ready access to information on service charges. Agency service representatives may not be familiar with the context in which the charges for a specific account were developed. Even when an agency is able to provide an apparently coherent statement of the service charges on an account, it is prudent to confirm the figures. The information provided by the agency may not be comprehensive and it may be based on assumptions that differ from those used by the library.

Comprehensiveness can be an issue. Despite agency efforts to provide consolidated annual invoices, publisher rate changes do not coordinate with agency billing cycles. It is almost inevitable that some unanticipated changes will occur during the year. Agencies usually pass these increases on to libraries in the form of supplemental invoices. Supplemental invoices also accrue as a library adds new titles to its list throughout the year and when publishers produce special issues or additional volumes at an additional charge. Unless a library and its supplier have a specific agreement about the fees applied to supplemental billings, there can be significant variations between these charges and those on the consolidated invoice. All invoices should be inspected to identify service charge calculations.

There may be variations in the fees levied for handling different types of serials materials. An agency may apply different service charges to: domestic and foreign serials; expensive and lower priced titles; high discount, low discount, and gratis publications; and periodical serials and non-periodical serials such as continuations and monographs in series. For instance, an agency may calculate the service charge on priced periodical serials as a percentage of the subscription price and apply different percentages to domestic and foreign titles. Within this structure, there may be a limit to the charge that accrues to any individual title. Non-periodical serials, gratis materials, and government publications may be excluded from the percentage charge and instead carry a fixed dollar-per-line service fee. Or, the percentage approach may apply to these items and be supplemented by a line charge; the line charge may be included in the price on which the percentage charge is based, or it may be added after the percentage charge is calculated. Shipping and handling fees levied for non-periodical materials forwarded by an agency may be excluded from service fee calculations, or they may attract charges at the standard percentage rate. None of these approaches is inherently right or wrong. What is important, however, is an awareness of the range of industry practices and the approaches applied to a specific account.

Percentage comparisons of the service charges of different vendors can be affected by differences in the ways agencies interpret or present the list prices of specific serials titles. Although significant variations are most common in the posting of prices for foreign publications and non-periodical serials, they can also occur in the listing of prices for domestic periodical serials. The subscription price and the dollar-per-line charge for handling certain types of serials may appear as separate items on the listings produced by one agency; another agency with the same pricing approach may combine the two and show them as a single charge. Percentage service charge evaluations of the two listings may produce significantly different results. The approach used by an agency can be confirmed by spot-checking the subscription prices shown on invoices against the prices shown in current issues of the titles and on publishers' renewal notices.

More variables operate in the presentation of subscription prices for foreign titles. Communication difficulties can adversely affect the accuracy of the subscription rate information available to agencies, and currency conversions add to the complexity of citing subscription prices. Agencies differ in how they apply and calculate foreign exchange. One may use the exchange rate in force when the agency pays the publisher, another may use the rate at the time the library's invoice is prepared, and yet another may use the rate in effect on the day payment is received from the library. Subscription agencies rarely lose money on foreign titles; potential losses from inaccurate subscription prices and variations in foreign exchange rates are recovered through supplemental billings. [It appears to be less common for agencies to voluntarily issue credits when the actual exchange rates are more favorable than those cited in the initial invoice.]

As with domestic materials, variations may be introduced in the charge a library identifies as the subscription price by an agency's assignment of line item charges for expenses such as foreign bank drafts. Agencies vary in their approaches for assessing charges for bank drafts. Some levy the full cost of a draft against every title despite the fact that the majority of subscription renewals are batched and only new orders are likely to be processed individually with each incurring the full cost of a draft. Such pricing practices do not necessarily show up in agency quotations for handling foreign serials; instead, they become evident only when a library inspects its consolidated and bill-back invoices and compares the subscription prices on these lists with the publisher's price using the exchange rate in force at the time orders were renewed. Libraries that subscribe to numerous foreign titles or expensive foreign titles can find it informative to compare actual invoiced costs for specific titles from libraries that use different vendors.

Reflecting publishers' diverse approaches to pricing and payment mechanisms for non-periodical serials, vendors employ a wide variety of pricing and invoicing procedures for these titles. [Continuations in agency parlance.] The picture is further complicated by the fact that publication schedules for these materials are often less than regular. Libraries that want to ensure that they receive all issues of non-periodical serials titles usually request that agencies place standing orders for these materials, that is, open orders that remain in force until actively cancelled by the library. While some publishers accommodate such orders, many do not. To meet library requirements, agencies establish internal procedures to manage order placement and payment for these titles as if they were standing orders. When standing orders are included on agency renewal lists and consolidated invoices, library managers should check that all pieces paid on previous invoices have been received before authorizing payment for additional pieces. [In the interests of not sending "good money after bad" this approach should be followed for all serials materials, including standard subscriptions. Any titles that are seriously behind in their publishing schedules should be investigated before being approved for renewal.]

Most libraries require that non-periodical serials serviced by an agency appear on their renewal lists and consolidated invoices to facilitate order confirmation, and budget allocation and planning. However, few of these titles require prepayment at the time of ordering; payment is due when publishers issue invoices, usually after dispatch of the "issues". In many cases, neither publication schedules nor prices can be determined in advance. Some agencies list these titles as "bill-later" items, indicating that prices cannot be determined and the material will be billed on supplemental invoices at the appropriate time. Others show the price for the most recent issue. In some cases, the actual prices or price estimates for bill-later titles will be included in the amount of the total invoice, resulting in inadvertent prepayment by the library. Agency billing practices for such materials should be clarified in pre-service negotiations. Such materials may or may not also be included in an agency's service charge calculations.

Agency-specific variations in the pricing of continuations may include different approaches to shipping and shipping charges. Many publishers of continuation titles offer vendors a choice in distribution methods. The titles can be handled like periodical serials—drop shipped from the publisher to the library—or dispatched to the vendor in bulk for reshipping to libraries. Some publishers offer additional discounts for orders shipped to a vendor in bulk. Vendors who choose to reship materials incur handling and shipping charges which are usually billed to the library; taxes may also be assigned on materials re-shipped to certain locations. While some vendors show these items as separate charges on their invoices, other do not, including them as part of the subscription price. If folded-in in this way, such charges may be included in service fee calculations. From a library's perspective, reshipping has some advantages. These include ready access to agency information on the publication status of such titles, the availability of packing slips to identify the source of the materials, and avoidance of the invoicing problems that can arise when publishers invoice a library for material for which it has or will pay the vendor.

What Services Are Covered? When comparing service charges among different vendors and different accounts, it is important to know what services are covered by the charges, so that the library is comparing apples with apples rather than with oranges or chickens.

Before the widespread introduction of general service charges, agents used a variety of mechanisms to add to the revenues they received from publisher discounts. These included charges for renewing the titles on a library's list, charges for processing new orders, charges for "rush" service, and charges for canceling subscriptions. Some also levied handling charges on materials on which they received no discounts. After the introduction of general service fees, some agencies retained elements of this charging structure, continuing to add an extra fee for handling government publications and other special materials, or levying additional fees for new subscriptions or rush orders. Others have retained cancellation fees.

Today, it is generally accepted that the service charge or handling fee covers the basic agency services of order placement, renewal, invoicing, claiming, claims reporting, and simple management report generation. Some smaller agencies quote different service fees for different levels of service: for example, one charge for order placement and renewal, and a higher fee for placement, renewal, *and* claim processing. Some agencies include access to electronic mail and online ordering and claiming in their handling fee, while others charge extra for such access.

As in so many aspects of subscription agency service to libraries, practices vary among agents and within agencies. The best way to determine what services an agency includes under the umbrella of its general service or handling fee is to ask. The question needs to be posed positively and negatively. Questions might include: "What services are provided as part of the basic subscription service?" "What services attract additional charges?" "What about . . .?". An awareness of the charging structures of several agents can be helpful in pricing and service negotiations. Such competitive information may provide the leverage either to persuade an agency to throw in a service for which it usually levies an added charge but which a competitor offers as part of its standard service or to lower the fee charged to an account.

Service Use and Service Fees: There are many reasons why two libraries which subscribe to similar titles and make similar use of agency services might pay different service charges to the same vendor. They include library sensitivity to costs, the negotiating skills of library personnel, and vendor competition. In some cases, differences in service fees result from differences in the libraries' use of agency services. Such differences are not necessarily obvious to the outside observer, and they may become such an accepted part of a library's operations that managers and staff forget to mention them when discussing service charges with colleagues or an alternate service provider. Among the variables that can impact on general service charges are the timing of a library's payment to its vendor (discounts for early payment, penalties for late payment) and special arrangements such as a vendor agreeing to issue only a single consolidated invoice and to absorb all charges that would normally be covered by supplemental invoices.

Equally, libraries with similar lists and obvious variations in their use of an agency's services may pay significantly different service charges, or they may not. Similar variables such as concern, clout, and competition operate when two libraries with similar lists and use of services pay different charges. An agency's formal pricing structure will also be influential when a library uses services that an agency bills separate from its standard service fee. The services that are most frequently billed separately are those relating to automation: online access to agencies' automated systems; use of remote check-in systems; and stand-alone products and services such as PC-based serials check-in systems and CD-ROM products. Even when an agency has a separate formal pricing structure for these services, a library can still negotiate to obtain a full or partial reduction in these charges:

> How much . . . an agent will provide and how much will be done without additional cost depends largely on the company's willingness to please the customer, that is, how much the vendor wants the library's business. One agency may provide a great number of services at no charge but be unwilling to do something slightly different for a single library. Another agency may charge for certain services but be quite flexible in what it will do for an individual customer, both for a fee and at no charge.[71]

Few agencies systematically monitor individual library usage of basic subscription services. Variations in the use of standard services are not usually reflected in service charge calculations:

> Typically, the service load imposed by a library is not well measured on an individual basis and is not much of a factor in the setting of price. . . The inefficient library can indeed cost the agency . . . more . . .[72]

While formal mechanisms are generally lacking, agents may build in a trouble factor when pricing lists for clients known to be particularly inefficient or demanding. An inefficient library is one that causes unnecessary work for an agency. For instance, a library that uses untrained personnel in claiming may generate a large number of claims that could have been avoided if the library's records were inspected more carefully. An extreme example is reported by Greene:

> . . . [a] library put in an emergency call to its agent that the library was having terrible trouble. "It has never happened before. Forty-five subscriptions aren't arriving. What's the matter with us?" The agent went to the library, took the claims, went over in the corner with *Ulrich's*, and started to go through the claims. The first twelve were bimonthly or quarterly. These subscriptions were all claimed back to January of 1972 for nonreceipt. The library did not keep historical records. The agent then went to the stacks. The first ten picked

up had a January cover date, but the earliest receiving date on any one of these issues was March. The majority of them were April.[73]

Each claim handled by an agency adds to its costs and the cost of servicing the account which originated the claim. Similarly, a library that dickers over its invoice for months but will not accept late payment charges and libraries that change agents every second year are more expensive to service than other libraries.

A library that makes little use of a service that its agent provides as part of its basic subscription service can negotiate for a lower fee or for substitution of a desired service for which the agency usually levies an additional charge. For example, a library that lacks the staff to survey check-in records for missing issues will make little use of agency support for claiming, as will a library that prefers to bypass agency claim support and forwards claims direct to publishers.

The Title Mix: When asked about the cost of servicing a potential customer's account, agency responses almost invariably include a conditional phrase identifying the title mix of the account as a significant factor in pricing. The title mix affects publisher discounts, agency margins, and the general levels of service charge an agency seeks to obtain in a particular market segment. Although agency systems have the potential to flag titles that are troublesome, and therefore costly to service, this information is rarely used systematically in setting service charges.[74]

What is a troublesome title? From an agency's point of view, a troublesome title is one that requires an above average degree of agency intervention: for example, a title, such as a mass-market magazine handled by a fulfillment house with a history of being unresponsive to library needs, that generates a high proportion of claims; titles from publishers who routinely change subscription rates more than once a year necessitating extra payment and invoicing cycles; or titles that rarely appear on schedule, causing high levels of claim activity. Non-periodical serials such as continuations also require high levels of agency intervention:

> Continuation titles fall among those which an agent considers "difficult," so if an account is made up predominantly of continuations it should come as no surprise if the handling charge on the account is high.[75]

A vendor alert to the cost of handling troublesome titles may use this awareness to obtain a larger proportion of a library's business:

To induce a vendor to handle a certain type of problem order, you may need to create a larger account by adding "standard" titles to the order mix.[76]

There is little relationship between the amount of effort an agency expends on servicing a title and its subscription price:

> The *Journal of Organometallic Chemistry* may cost twenty times as much as *Popular Science*, but the cost to the agent of handling those journals is rather similar. What creates costs for the agent is the extent of handling involved with a title. If the agent must communicate with the publisher to find out why the April issue has already appeared when the March issue has not, then next communicate this information to the library customers, etc. then that title will be an expensive title for the agent to handle. A journal's handling cost to the agent is a direct and inverse function of the degree of professionalism and reliability of the journal's publisher. A journal that appears every month is a joy. A journal that appears monthly during term (whose term time?), and bi-monthly otherwise, but with a double issue at Whitsuntide and occasional and highly irregular supplements, and is chronically behind schedule and irregularly so, is as much a bane to the agent as it is to the librarian.[77]

The Account Environment: All of the factors discussed in this chapter are taken into consideration when an agency establishes the service fee for a particular account. Agency viability depends upon the sum of its cumulative decisions on the fees levied on individual accounts. The objective is to price services at a level that is acceptable to the market while meeting agency margin objectives. Each agency knows the range of its own margin objectives; what it needs to determine are the tolerances and priorities of its clients and potential clients.

Vendors devote a great deal of time and effort to monitoring the serials acquisitions practices of libraries. The affiliations of very large accounts are watched closely, with the attention aficionados devote to the latest subplots in *Days of Our Lives* or the progress of the Chicago Bears. Rumors abound and are seized with alacrity by competing vendors. Word that the serials manager at library X has expressed dissatisfaction with the service it receives from vendor Y can have quite dramatic effects if the account is sufficiently large or prestigious. A deluge of phone calls and offers from interested vendors and personal visits from senior staff of the agency currently holding the account will follow. News that library X has actually switched its account from vendor Y to vendor Z is treated as a major victory by vendor Z and used as a marketing tool to attract other clients. Staff of abandoned vendor Y analyze the loss, re-examine internal procedures, and work furiously on damage control to prevent the loss of other clients likely to be influenced by the defection. While only the largest or most influential accounts attract industry-wide attention, agency marketing personnel and sales representatives monitor libraries in their local constituencies with similar attentiveness.

Agencies use standard approaches to establish contact and develop relationships with potential customers: national, regional, and market segment sales representatives, direct mail, telemarketing, advertising, participation in professional associations, conference exhibits, etc. Once contact is established, an agency sets out to examine a number of issues: how the library currently acquires its serials; the likelihood of effecting a change —from ordering direct to ordering through an agent, from ordering through agent Y to ordering through agent Z, or from ordering through multiple agents to consolidating orders with agent Z; and the desirability of effecting a change—the costs the agency will incur in handling the account versus the price the library is prepared to pay for the service.

In contact with the library through personal visits or phone calls, agency personnel probe for signals that indicate the library's priorities. Is cost the primary concern? Access to machine readable bibliographic records? Agency support for claiming? Which aspects of current service generate negative comments and which receive acclaim? Where is the competition vulnerable? Do staff say that cost is the primary concern, and yet complain about not being visited by vendor representatives or the lack of availability of a link between the vendor's automated system and the local library system? How realistic are the library's expectations? Would any vendor be able to meet them?

Assessing the account. Is the account worth pursuing? Can it be switched from the current vendor and, if so, would it be worth the effort? How big is the account? Can the size of the account be increased by consolidating orders from multiple vendors, by including subscriptions for branch or departmental locations, or by adding the individual subscriptions of corporate personnel? Is the library able to commit to a supplier for a multi-year term? Does the library have a need for services over and above basic subscription management (services for which the agency levies an additional charge or for which the representative receives an additional bonus)? If there is no current interest in such services, can such an interest be developed? Does the library use an automated library system? A serials check-in system? Which systems? Does it plan to install such systems in the future?

Collection characteristics. What are the characteristics of the library's serials list? Is it standard for its market segment, or does it include materials that are not usually found in a library of that size and type? Does the library support unique or unusual programs that require foreign language materials, newsletters, or serials from alternative publishers? Does the collection have a high number of multiple copy orders? Which materials cause the greatest problems for the library? How many non-periodical serials does the library receive? Will these be included in the list to be serviced by an agent? What about memberships? Does the library have policies which limit placing orders with an agent, ordering high-priced titles direct from the publisher, or requiring that lists be split among multiple agencies?

Service requirements. What are the basic service requirements of the account? Are there multiple ship-to and billing addresses? Special financial coding requirements? Do subscriptions follow a standard calendar year term? Does the library have an unusual schedule for renewals and invoicing? Does the library process and pay invoices promptly? Will the library expect a lower service charge for early payment? Will it accept late payment charges if payment is delayed beyond thirty days after the invoice is received?

What form of title does the library use on orders and claims? What form of title does it require on invoices, renewal lists, and other documentation? What other reports does the library expect to receive? How many copies of each report? Are there any special requirements as to the order of items in reports? Does the library use agency support for claiming, or does it place claims direct with publishers? How many claims does the library generate? What level of staff prepare claims? Are claims reviewed before dispatch?

What special or additional services are required? Will the library accept direct charges for additional services, or does it expect these to be covered by the service fee? What is the library's experience of other agents?

Working contacts. Who makes decisions about the library's suppliers—the staff member being interviewed, that person's supervisor, the library director, the board, or a procurement officer? What are the concerns, objectives, and prejudices of the decision maker? Can the agency establish contact with the decision maker without slighting the person with whom the initial contact has been made? What influence does the current contact have with the decision maker?

While seeking information about the library and its account, the agency representative will also present information and answer questions about the agency, its services, and procedures. A skilled presenter will shape the presentation to stress features and services that address issues of importance to the library. While not necessarily making overt comparisons with the service and performance of other vendors, the representative will seek to demonstrate the superiority of the agency being represented. In situations in which an agency knows it is in competition with another vendor, the comparisons may be more direct.

How Agencies Calculate Service Charges: If a potential account interests an agency, the agency will make a firm price proposal. In most agencies, pricing is an art rather than a science. Once again, there are no set procedures, only general practices.

Most agencies assemble price quotes by market sector, based on the agency's knowledge of the types of serials in the collections of different types of libraries, its average margins on these materials, and its current margin objective for that sector of the market. Computer generated averages based on the agency's existing client list are used to determine the amounts the agency can expect to remit to publishers and the margins it achieves on such titles. These factors determine the range within which pricing for a particular account will be established. Within this range, the quote for a specific list will be adjusted to meet the perceived requirements of the account—the priorities of the library, competition from other agencies, and the library's negotiating stance.

It is costly to use automated agency systems to develop quotes for potential clients. The subscription price and agency margin must be checked for each title and discrepancies between the list and the agency's files detected and resolved. Such effort is infrequently rewarded; agencies rarely obtain ten percent of the business on which they quote. Quotes for existing accounts can be generated automatically as the data is already in the agent's system.

MISCELLANEOUS INCOME

Although it represents only a small proportion of total revenues, income from miscellaneous sources can have a major impact on agency profitability. Miscellaneous income is the only revenue source in which an agent's activities are not limited by competitive forces. No matter how good an agency's relations are with publishers or how well it negotiates with them, the levels of discount it obtains will be limited by what publishers establish as their norms for discounts to subscription agencies. No matter how superior an agent's subscription services are to libraries or how insensitive its market is to costs, the extent of the service charges it can levy will be limited by competition from other agencies. Outside of miscellaneous income, the only other area in which creative management can significantly impact agency profitability is internal cost containment.

Not all sources of miscellaneous income are created equal. To have the potential to boost profitability above industry averages, a revenue source must be accessible without major development or marketing efforts and unfettered by price competition from other agencies. Such conditions do not apply to automated products and services for libraries and publishers; they do prevail in areas such as short-term money management and catalog advertising. In a small agency, the aggressive sale of advertising space in title catalogs can contribute as much as a third of the company's pre-tax profits. In large agencies, equally aggressive money management can generate revenues equal to half the agency's pre-tax profit.

AGENCY EFFICIENCY

All other things being equal, an efficient, well-managed agency is better placed to compete in the library marketplace than is an inefficient agency. Assessment of agency efficiency is highly subjective. Within agencies, the criteria for assessing efficiency will vary with agency objectives. Profit is clearly an important objective in most agencies. However, the expression of the profit objective will vary, as will the relative importance of profit against other objectives. An agency might aim to be the largest agency or the predominant supplier to a particular segment of the market. Another agency may focus on being recognized as the leading provider of automated support for libraries. Objectives vary from agency to agency, within one agency over time, and among individuals within one agency at the same time.

Agency objectives impact both efficiency criteria and overhead costs. An agency that operates on the assumption that there is a market for low cost, no frills subscription services is likely to be extremely cost conscious in its internal operations and to minimize its expenditures on exhibit booths and client entertainment. An agency that believes that libraries with large serials budgets are attracted to vendors with sophisticated automation capabilities will invest more heavily in research and development than an agency targeting the school library market. Thus, a library seeking to obtain serial services at lowest cost should look for an agency that targets the cost sensitive segment of the library market. A library looking for sophisticated library-oriented automated service support in addition to basic subscription handling should expect to pay a premium for the added services.

THE FUTURE OF SUBSCRIPTION AGENCIES

During the 1980s, the number of North American subscription agencies continued to decrease with smaller agencies going out of business or being absorbed by larger agencies. Several European companies expanded their activities through the purchase of smaller U.S. companies. EBSCO and Faxon retained their position as the largest agencies, both within North America and internationally. The strength of the current players appears to have limited significant advances in the penetration of other European agencies into the North American market. Book dealers will continue to be a substantial source of service for non-periodical serials.

No significant new agencies emerged during the decade, and the potential for new vendors appears to be low. While librarians lament the concentration of subscription agency services in the hands of a few large players, their service expectations have increased to the point where it would be prohibitively expensive for a new agency to enter the league of major players. In the most cost-sensitive market segments, there may be potential for smaller specialized vendors offering a limited range of services designed specifically for the target market. Such vendors would need to focus on operational efficiency and cost containment to be able to compete effectively against the large, full-service general agencies.

There are indications that economic pressures will direct more attention to agency services and service charges than previously. Even though some libraries appear reluctant to address this issue, their parent organizations and governing authorities are becoming increasingly aware of the costs of serials and are anxious to explore methods of reducing or containing costs. In recent years increased cost sensitivity has spurred price competition among vendors. In the view of one agent,

> . . . agent competition is holding down service charge rates to artificial levels. At present, agents are sometimes more concerned with gaining market share than with making profit on an account.[78]

If these pressures continue, agencies may counter by reviewing their laissez-faire approach to service usage as a determinant of service charges. Cost-sensitive libraries may also contribute to this review. Libraries that make little use of services such as claiming and online access to agency files may seek reductions in service charges for their non-use of "standard" services and express reluctance to subsidize provision of these service to other libraries.

There appears to be little immediate likelihood of major new developments in the automated services agencies offer libraries. During the 1980s, the automated services which had been the preserve of the larger agencies—online access to agency files and interfaces between agency systems and library systems—became the norm for all but the smallest vendors. The larger agencies have shifted their development focus to areas more remote from day-to-day subscription management such as electronic publishing in online and CD-ROM formats. Services to publishers can be expected to increase slowly as more publishers implement automated systems capable of being linked to agency systems. The relatively humble technology of facsimile may have the greatest impact on publisher-agency-library relationships because it offers rapid communications without requiring substantial technological expertise or investment.

Libraries with sophisticated local automated serials control systems may find agency support for the acquisition of periodical serials less attractive than previously. Those with relatively stable subscription lists and the ability to issue multiple checks in a timely fashion may choose to purchase serials direct from publishers. The alacrity with which such a move occurs can be expected to be greater in institutions where administrative concern for serials expenditures and agency service charges is accompanied by pressure to justify the significant purchase and maintenance costs of local automated library systems. Libraries that are constrained by complex financial procedures may choose to retain agency services but at a reduced level, using agencies only for order placement and invoice consolidation, and handling claiming and report generation (covering all serials materials from all sources, not just those from a single vendor) in-house. The reduced use of standard agency services can be expected to generate pressure for reduced handling fees on these accounts.

4 CHOOSING AN AGENCY

There is no magic formula that will ensure that a library selects the best vendor to service its serials acquisitions needs. A satisfactory selection requires that a library define its needs and priorities, identify and evaluate the agencies willing and able to meet these needs, and negotiate appropriate service and pricing agreements. The formality of the process varies. Some libraries are required to seek bids based on written statements of needs and a formal evaluation and award process. Others use a less formal approach to survey their options in response to perceived non-performance by a current vendor or to follow up an apparently attractive offer from another vendor. For many serials managers, agency selection is a non-linear and ongoing process in which the manager continuously monitors the library's needs and priorities against the serials supply environment and progressively adjusts the service mix between the library and its agents.

Critical thought is the element most essential to successful vendor selection. All assumptions about the library's needs, vendors' services, and the fit between them must be identified and questioned. Too many serials supply decisions are based on the unquestioning application of conventional wisdoms, which may be neither conventional nor wise.

This chapter addresses the definition of service needs and the selection of appropriate vendors. Much of the discussion is presented in terms that suggest both a formal selection process and selection of a single supplier. This approach is merely one of convenience; libraries that follow less structured vendor selection procedures and those that seek to identify more than one vendor to support their needs will find that most of the material is also relevant to their situations.

DIRECT ORDERING FROM PUBLISHERS

Despite the prevailing wisdom that all but the smallest library can benefit from using subscription agencies or other vendor support for serials acquisitions, local circumstances can be such that larger libraries may also choose to order all titles direct from publishers. In libraries with limited lists of serials, the workload of ordering direct may be absorbed by staff borrowed from other duties or the major clerical load may fall on an organizational unit outside of the library.

Most libraries obtain at least *some* of their serials direct from publishers. The most common reason for ordering direct is to obtain publications that are not available in any other way. A surprisingly large number of major publishers will not accept orders from agencies, preferring to deal direct with client libraries. Some publishers will accept agency orders for foreign libraries but not for domestic libraries. And some publishers will accept agency orders for some titles but not for others. H. W. Wilson, a major supplier of periodical abstracting and indexing services, will not accept agency orders for domestic library subscriptions. R.R. Bowker will accept agency orders for *Library Journal* but not for its periodical directories. Reader's Digest does not accept orders from agencies. Some CD-ROM publishers accept agency orders, others do not. University Microfilms International accepts only direct orders. A number of publishers of serials services, particularly those focussing on business and investment, do not accept orders from agencies, nor do many publishers of controlled circulation magazines. Some national societies, institutions, and associations will only deal with members; some allow institutional memberships handled by third parties, others do not; and still others will not support anything other than direct individual memberships.

Subscription agencies also impose restrictions on the materials they handle. The most obvious case is titles available "free on request." Traditionally, subscription agencies have not handled gratis publications such as trade magazines or corporate annual reports. This approach originated before the introduction of service charges when agencies were not comfortable levying direct handling fees on non-priced publications. At least one agency has discovered that there is a market for subscription agency management of gratis materials and will process orders for unpriced serials for a handling fee of approximately $8.00 per title. As most agencies do not offer such a service, libraries generally order gratis material direct from publishers.

Librarians routinely report difficulties in finding subscription agents specializing in exotic publications: serials published in certain languages or geographic regions, fugitive materials, avant garde literary magazines, and underground and counterculture titles. There are competent agencies specializing in some of these materials, but it can be difficult, frustrating, and expensive to locate them. By and large, subscription agencies are best able to handle the ordinary commercial serials that present few problems for libraries. Many librarians recognize this fact, and use agencies for the tasks they perform best, reserving in-house resources to manage the acquisition of problem titles direct from publishers:

> . . . what agents do best is precisely what is easiest for the serials librarian to do: enter, renew and claim mainstream domestic periodicals. . . . The service we would most like to buy is the least likely to be available for sale; the service the librarian can most easily procure in-house is the service most commonly offered for sale. The most popular resolution of this dichotomy is to place most paid subscriptions with agents and reserve the true horrors to be dealt with in-house. By assigning the great number of routine subscriptions to the agent, we allow ourselves to devote time in-house to dealing with publishers known or suspected to deviate from standard publishing schedules, to be less reliable in maintaining subscription lists, or to be generally more likely to pose problems with renewal, receipt, and claiming.[79]

Many libraries find it more convenient to deal directly with small local publishers than to impose a third party in the relationship. When reserving problem titles for in-house management, library managers are making cost-benefit judgements; they expect to experience difficulties no matter what the method of acquisition but judge that the effort involved in straightening out problems will be less if they deal directly with publishers.

The pursuit of more obvious cost savings may also cause libraries to place orders for expensive titles direct with publishers. If an agency calculates service fees as a flat percentage of subscription prices with no dollar limit on the charge for an individual title, a library may decide to handle its own orders for expensive titles to limit the amount spent on service charges. Similar logic may apply if a library acquires a number of high ticket titles from a single publisher and is able to obtain a discount by ordering direct, or if similarly significant savings are available for the direct purchase of material published by a library's parent institution or affiliate.

Serials management will be facilitated if a library develops guidelines to determine when to place orders direct with publishers and when to channel them through subscription agencies or other vendors. The guidelines may be simple. For example, a library may order direct only material that cannot be obtained through the library's primary subscription agency. Alternatively, the guidelines may be more complex, as in the guidelines developed by the University of California at Irvine:

. . . order directly from publishers: (a) out of necessity, when the publisher accepted only direct orders; (b) expensive publications, to avoid costly service charges (our cutoff figure was $400 per subscription); (c) to take advantage of substantial discounts offered by publishers on expensive titles; (d) when known factors of service favored ordering directly from publishers; (e) local publications; and (f) titles published by [the parent institution] which could be "recharged" through a transfer of funds within the university. The remainder . . . place with agents if they [can] service the titles.[80]

To achieve optimum service when ordering direct, library staff should approach the task with the zeal of the ideal subscription agency, exploring all aspects of publishers' ordering procedures and subscription rates. The information to be assembled should include:

- publisher name, address, telephone, and fax numbers,
- contact points for subscription placement and service problems,
- availability of toll-free telephone number,
- bibliographic information on title(s): frequency, associated publications, special issues, indexes,
- basic subscription rate, availability of special subscription rates— for members, for purchase of multiple titles, multiple copies, for multi-year subscriptions, for other package deals,
- coverage of subscription: main title only, supplements, special issues, indexes, etc.,
- procedures for notifying availability of special issues, supplements, etc.,
- procedures for obtaining special issues,
- subscription terms supported: calendar year only, volume only, short-term (less than one year) subscriptions, odd term (one year plus x months) subscriptions,
- lead time required to activate subscription,
- procedures to implement subscription: payment must accompany order, invoice issued after receipt of order, etc.,
- currency requirements,
- procedures for notifying and implementing subscription rate changes,
- procedures for claiming missing issues, replacing damaged issues, time limit for claims, address for claims, ordering and payment information to be submitted with claims,
- procedures for cancelling or changing order, cancellation refund policy, time limit on cancellations,

- renewal procedures and deadlines,
- subscriber information/qualification requirements,
- procedures for handling multi-copy subscriptions, multiple delivery addresses, different ship-to and billing addresses.

If a library decides to place a direct order for a title it previously received through an agency, it should also check with the publisher to confirm the expiration date of its current subscription. Publishers' records do not necessarily accord with those of agencies and libraries, and gaps or duplicates can result if the library fails to determine the appropriate start date for the new subscription. Additionally, the library should inform the publisher that its order is a renewal of the subscription previously handled by agency X.

SINGLE OR MULTIPLE AGENCIES?

While united on the benefits of using subscription agencies, librarians and vendors often differ on whether a library should place all of its titles with a single agency or use the services of multiple vendors. Agents usually argue that it is best for a library to place its orders with a single vendor citing benefits that include: simplified communication, uniform workflows, pricing or service charge discounts, and consolidated management reports covering all of the library's titles. However, vendors' marketing tactics vary. An agency will usually try to obtain *all* of a library's business. If this is not practical—as when a library has a firm commitment to using multiple vendors, or has subscription needs that can only be serviced by a specialist vendor—agencies almost always accept such business as they can get.

Many librarians agree on placing all orders with a single vendor:

> For many libraries the ideal situation is to place all serial orders, including both subscriptions and standing orders, with one vendor, particularly if the list of orders is relatively standard and predominantly American. The only orders not placed with the agent would be those for which the publisher will not accept orders from agents, such as the H. W. Wilson Company titles. This consolidation permits the library to process the fewest number of invoices and to deal with only one agency. If the vendor's computers compile management data, that information will be more useful than if the orders

are divided among several sources, since it will include nearly all of a library's current serial orders. Claims could, with few exceptions, be sent to one source.[81]

But most recognize that such an approach is reliable only when the library has a relatively standard serials collection:

> Both the proportion of a library's orders placed through agents and the number of agents used depend upon the size and scope of the collection. Small libraries and special libraries can perhaps work with a single vendor successfully. Their titles are limited either numerically, geographically, or by subject. Academic and research libraries, on the other hand, have more complex serials collections and may have better results employing more than one agent.[82]

Large research libraries typically use multiple agents to service their accounts. Of seventy-four major academic research libraries surveyed by Derthick and Moran in 1985,[83] 99 percent used more than one agency, three percent used two agents, and 69 percent used more than seven agents. The number of agents used by a single library ranged from one to sixty; the average number of agents used by each library was seventeen. These findings contrast with a study of a similar population by Huff in 1970.[84] Of the 49 libraries surveyed by Huff, 43 used more than one agent, 20 used two agents, and only four used more than seven agents.

A major reason for the use of multiple agents is their varying expertise in handling different types of material:

> Every agent has strengths and weaknesses, and it is to the library's advantage to recognize and use an agency's strengths. Variables to be considered are type of material (journals or non-periodical serials), subject of material, and geographic location of the publisher. Some vendors restrict themselves to, for example, standing orders, a single language, or scientific serials—whatever they do best. Many others will accept an order for any title and do their best to supply it. This is commendable, but a library with a strong collection of German or African serials should have more success with a vendor in the country of origin, or at least one specializing in that region, than with a general domestic subscription agency.[85]

Derthick and Moran found that libraries that wanted to use more agencies were not only seeking better service for specific

CHOOSING AN AGENCY **91**

types of publications, but were also interested in spreading their business to maintain competition and the quality of service and to reduce the impact of any problems that might arise from the deterioration of an agency's service or the failure of an agency:

> We have also found it not to be a good idea to have everything with one vendor as takeovers/sellouts do occur . . . and this can cause not merely headaches, but large losses of library money as well.[86]

A library that uses a subscription agency is vulnerable. If the agency fails to provide competent service, the library will suffer. Problems can include breaks in supply due to late placement of orders or renewals, gaps due to inadequate processing of claims, confusion over shipping and billing addresses, and even receipt of the wrong publication. Such problems can be difficult, labor intensive, tedious, and expensive to resolve.

Agencies can also go bankrupt. If this happens after a library has paid for its subscriptions but before the agency has processed and paid for the library's orders and renewals, the library can lose its money with little chance of recovering it. In practice, such spectacular failures are rare among mainstream agencies. Splitting orders among multiple agencies can limit the risk, since the failure of one agency would threaten only a portion of the library's serials budget. However, it can also increase a library's exposure by linking it to the economic health of more than one agency. Neither agency size nor reputation guarantee against business failure. A library concerned to protect itself against such risks can require that an agency take out a performance bond, or it can negotiate an agreement whereby it does not pay an agency until it has received proof of payment for its subscriptions. Performance bonds add to the cost of a vendor doing business and are not considered cost effective for amounts of less than $50,000.[87] Both approaches can increase the service charges for handling an account.

LIBRARY NEEDS AND PRIORITIES

Libraries and subscription agencies do not communicate by telepathy. The only way an agency will know that its offer to service a library's serials subscriptions is expected to include multiple re-newal lists arranged alphabetically by title for each of five ship-to locations and three copies of a consolidated renewal list arranged by library-assigned financial code is if the library has:

- analyzed its operations and determined that it needs this list in these formats, and
- communicated this need to the agency.

To make a rational choice between an agency that is unable to provide the reports in the requested formats, one that will supply the reports within its standard service fee, and one that will generate the reports for an additional annual fee, the library must also have:

- assigned the renewal list (or other) requirement a priority that reflects its relative importance vis-a-vis other operational requirements, and
- determined the place of operational requirements in the hierar-chy of the library's other criteria for agency selection, including cost and quality of service.

Renewal lists are hardly a pivotal point for the success of a library-agency relationship or the financial health of a vendor. But consid-er the effect on both library and agency of a library failing to communicate three or four similar but different special require-ments until an agency is managing the account. Library operations will be disrupted as will the agency's cost and profit projections, and neither the library nor the vendor is likely to have a positive perception of the other party.

As illustrated, clear definition and communication of library requirements is essential. Without such communication, the li-brary will not realize an appropriate return on its expenditures, and the long-term viability of the vendor will be threatened. While both parties benefit, responsibility for defining and communicat-ing service requirements rests with the library. An experienced vendor representative can assist a library in refining and articulat-ing its requirements in much the same way as a reference librarian probes a user's information needs when conducting a reference interview. However, the library cannot rely on such expert assistance being available and should not, in any case, abnegate its responsibility for determining its own needs and priorities.

PROFILING THE COLLECTION

Identify *all* serials the library acquires:

—those in the main collection and subsidiary collections
—subscriptions for individuals and nonlibrary locations
—periodicals and non-periodicals:

newspapers and newsletters
monographs in series
continuations
loose-leaf services
annual reports
and government publications

—and serials in all formats:

print
microform
CD-ROM
floppy disk
and computer files, as applicable.

The survey should also note any other resources controlled by the serials department—individual and corporate memberships, for instance—and any serials that are acquired through non-library channels.

The first step in needs definition is to profile the library's current serials collection. Identify *all* serials the library acquires: those in the main collection and subsidiary collections; subscriptions for individuals and nonlibrary locations; periodicals and non-periodicals: newspapers and newsletters, monographs in series, continuations, loose-leaf services, annual reports, and government publications; and serials in all formats: print, microform, CD-ROM, floppy disk, and computer files, as applicable. The survey should also note any other resources controlled by the serials department—individual and corporate memberships, for instance—and any serials that are acquired through nonlibrary channels.

Examine the acquisitions characteristics of the serials and categorize them accordingly. Depending on the collection, relevant groupings might include:

• periodicals—domestic and foreign
• newspapers—local, national, and foreign; print and microform
• controlled circulation publications
• non-priced materials
• publications received as gifts or through exchange
• titles known to be available only direct from the publisher
• monographs in series
• annuals and continuations
• serial services—loose-leaf services, abstracts and indexes
• memberships and association publications
• government publications—local, state, national, foreign, and international
• publications received on deposit, and
• serials in machine-readable formats.

Develop other categories and subcategories that may be appropriate to the particular collection. Such categories might include the output of publishers or organizations of special importance to the library's mission, materials from foreign countries or regions, and non-English-language materials.

Note the cost characteristics of the titles in the collection. This need not entail exhaustive record checking and analysis; the objective is to get a feel for the collection as a whole and to identify any major variations in the range of costs for different categories of materials. If there is a wide range in the cost of individual items in a category, note the most expensive titles and the range of costs for other titles. Estimate the rate of price increase in the collection as a whole, and identify any categories in which prices appear to be escalating more rapidly.

Examine the life cycle of the collection and sub-collections. In general, what are the changes that occur in the library's list, and what is the pattern of these changes? How many new titles are ordered each year, and how many are cancelled? Does the list grow, or must an existing title be cancelled if a new title is to be ordered? Is there a higher rate of change in specific materials categories, publication formats, or subject areas? Is there a core list of titles to which the library rarely makes changes? Are major changes in the list clustered in certain time periods—annually or once every three years—or do they occur all the time with no observable concentrations?

Also consider the subscription characteristics of the collection. How many multiple copy orders, multi-year subscriptions, and multiple ship-to and billing addresses are there? What is the frequency and nature of changes in these elements? Do such characteristics and changes apply to most materials or only to those in certain formats or categories?

Include any acquisitions problems. Again, look for patterns that relate to particular categories of material such as: lags in subscription renewals for titles from a particular source, high rates of missing issue claims for mass-market periodicals, frequent supplemental invoices for foreign titles, consistent supply of the wrong publication by a specific publisher, difficulties in tracking invoices for continuations, and consistent user complaints about the timeliness of receipt of loose-leaf services from a particular publisher or distributor. Note any terror titles that attract problems at every turn.

While reviewing the collection, also note any titles or categories of material critical to the library's mission and to the perceptions that users and managers have of the quality of library service. Take special care to ensure rapid and accurate supply of such materials. In an academically oriented senior high school, college catalogs could assume this status; in a business library, it might be the multiple copies of a daily trade paper or newsletter the library is responsible for distributing to officers; in a public library, a relatively obscure periodical beloved of the Board Chairman; and, in an academic library, the research publications in the field of interest to an influential department that is frequently critical of library performance.

THE ACQUISITIONS ENVIRONMENT

Next, consider the library and the organization of which it is part, the environment in which the collection is maintained and used. What are the current constraints and opportunities, and how can these be expected to change over time?

Is funding a problem? If so, it is a problem for the institution as a whole, for the library, or for serial purchases? Is there an institutional bias for or against expenditures on services that reduce staffing? Are the library or its parent institution sensitive to service charges? Are there formal or informal limits on the levels of service charges considered reasonable? Do library and institutional attitudes and concerns differ, and is there any indication that the current balance of power will change in the near future? Does the library have the ability to enter into multi-year service contracts? Would it be politically astute to exercise this option in the current climate?

Does the library have sufficient staff to handle current serials acquisitions? Is the staffing stable or subject to high turnover? Is turnover concentrated in specific positions? What impact does turnover have on existing procedures and performance? What recurring problems can be traced to turnover? Will turnover continue if staffing is reduced? Does the department have access to a pool of suitably qualified replacement personnel? Do students or volunteers form a significant part of the serials work force? Is this a permanent and/or required feature of the staffing structure? Do special problems arise because of part-time or temporary staff?

Do staff have experience in the use of subscription agencies? What are their attitudes and biases, and what are those of senior library administrators and managers? Is the department anticipating a change in key personnel? If an unanticipated change occurred, would that have a radical effect on current procedures, practices, attitudes, and needs?

Are users satisfied with current acquisitions procedures? Are there vocal groups or influential individuals with special requirements that *must* be met or who regularly complain about problems in the supply of specific titles or groups of materials? Do complaints relate to the method of acquisition, or are they inherent in the nature of the publication? What is the library doing to educate users about these problems?

Is the library and/or its parent institution automated? Is automation of acquisitions, serials, or accounting and finance planned for the future? How will this impact upon serials acquisitions? What are the reporting needs of management and the parent institution? Are reporting requirements stable or subject to constant change? Can the institution accept reports in machine-readable form?

What are the format requirements? Does the library have a commitment to provide serials data to other organizations? How does the library provide information on serials holdings to its users at the home site and in remote offices or branches?

What are management's current priorities? Do they include cost containment and curbs on staffing or is service to users paramount? How are these priorities interpreted by the library administration or the manager in charge of serials operations? Are the key managers, board members, or decision makers likely to change in the next several years? Would change result in a radical shift in priorities?

What serials subscription services does the library require in addition to order placement and renewal? Which services are essential, which are desirable but not mandatory, and which are of interest only if available at no extra charge? Services regarded as essential should be considered in detail. The consideration should include the definition of criteria for satisfactory vendor performance and mechanisms for monitoring performance.

AVAILABLE SERVICES

In theory, a library's definition of its serials acquisition service requirements need not be confined to the range of services currently offered by various suppliers. In practice, efficiency and the desire to achieve a workable fit between library and vendors demand that needs definition, prioritization, and vendor evaluation be undertaken within the broad constraints of the range of services actually offered by vendors. It is rare for a vendor to develop a major new service to meet the needs of a single library or a small group of libraries. If a vendor undertakes such development, it will seek to recover its costs from additional users, increased subscription business, direct billing of the library for which the capability was developed, or from general revenues derived from all customers. A library which requires a customized service may find its future options limited, being unable to abandon its investment to take advantage of more attractive pricing or services from another vendor.

All serials subscription vendors support a core of basic capabilities which include:

- provision of title, publisher, and pricing data,
- order placement, renewal, and cancellation services,
- retention and storage of order and payment records,
- assistance in the forwarding of claims to publishers,

- consolidation of renewal lists, invoices, and reports on claims, and
- flexibility in the formatting of standard reports.

Many vendors also provide auxiliary services that may be valuable in certain library situations. Among the more common auxiliary services are:

- serials check-in systems and services,
- online access to vendor information files,
- support for electronic ordering and claiming,
- machine-readable cataloging data,
- interfaces between vendor systems and local automated library systems, and
- electronic transmission of orders and claims to publishers.

Each vendor's services differ in detail, flexibility, and pricing.

An in-depth knowledge of the service offerings of several vendors can assist in defining library needs and priorities, evaluating vendor proposals, and negotiating with vendors. Comparisons between different vendors may highlight needs and opportunities that would otherwise be overlooked. Information on vendor services and pricing is readily available from vendor literature and service representatives, library literature, and the experience of other librarians.

The investigation of serials acquisitions support services should not be limited to the offerings of serials subscription agencies. Other vendors also provide services to support serials acquisitions; many libraries find that book jobbers offer competitive service for continuations and standing orders. In addition, some of the auxiliary services offered by subscription agencies are also available from other sources. For example, library automation companies offer automated serials management and check-in systems; online information services provide access to publisher name and address data and bibliographic information on serials; and bibliographic utilities and cataloging support services supply machine-readable cataloging data for serials.

ESTABLISHING PRIORITIES

A library will not reap the full benefit of the time and thought devoted to needs definition unless it also establishes criteria on which to base vendor selection. In some situations, selection priorities will be clear, mandated by the library's administrative authority, bid procedures, or the objective of a specific review situation. In other cases, the objectives of a vendor review, and thus selection or evaluation priorities, will be less obvious.

Almost everyone involved in needs assessment will have a clear understanding of the objective of the exercise; however, difficulties arise when each party's understanding is clear but different! The serials check-in clerk wants claim reports issued monthly with a separate report showing first claims to which the agency has received no response. The clerk's supervisor is focussed on finding a responsive supplier for the library's standing orders and continuations. The serials manager has a strong interest in agencies that can provide machine-readable invoices in a format that can be loaded to Lotus 1-2-3 for analysis and is also concerned to find a supplier who will guarantee no increase in service fee for three years. The library director feels pressure to cut staffing without diminishing service to users and wants to consolidate all orders with one agency and increase the proportion of orders placed with agencies. Although the institution served by the library has not been directly involved in the serials acquisition review, the library director anticipates that there will be no increase in funding for serials in the next budget.

The political success of any vendor selection decision will depend upon the manager's ability to define and prioritize selection criteria that reflect the concerns of all parties. In many cases, the primary criterion will be the objective which led to the review of supply arrangements, for example, the desire to maintain subscription agency service while limiting library expenditure on service charges. When a review or selection process originates from a less focussed desire to ensure that a library is making the best use of available options, selection criteria and priorities will emerge during the investigation. Consistency and commitment require that these criteria be formalized and presented to decision makers for validation *before* being applied in vendor selection.

Even when the basic objective is defined in the initial decision to undertake a review, precise criteria and priorities will still have to be established. Consider a review in which cost is the primary concern. How primary a concern is it? Is the library prepared to accept the lowest cost option regardless of all other factors? If not, what services *must* be provided before an agency will be considered? If cost is secondary to service, what levels of service is the library seeking? Is service the primary concern only up to specific cost ceiling? What is the ceiling? Are there specialized service requirements without which a vendor will not be considered? What is the library prepared to pay for such services?

CHALLENGING ASSUMPTIONS

When defining a library's serials acquisition needs, there is no substitute for plain old-fashioned thinking. It is essential that needs definition address the real needs of each individual library. Conventional wisdoms such as "online ordering benefits libraries," "large files of title information are essential to effective agency service," or "all libraries can benefit from agency claiming support" can be useful. They emphasize capabilities that other librarians (or vendors) consider relevant to most libraries. However, they become dangerous when accepted as expressing the needs of *all* libraries, or when adopted as sufficient expression of a single library's actual requirements. Loose investigation and definition of library needs will adversely affect the benefits a library obtains from agency services.

Close attention is also required when evaluating the extent to which a vendor's services meet the needs of a given library. The purchase of subscription agency services is a commercial transaction in which it is the library manager's responsibility to take all reasonable steps to ensure that the services offered meet the library's needs.

> Most library suppliers will not lie to the customer; they just do not necessarily tell the whole truth. The librarian's responsibility is to know what questions to ask to uncover more of the truth.[88]

This section examines some common assumptions about the serials acquisition services and capabilities sought by libraries and promoted by agencies. The intention is not to signal that the products and services described require more careful analysis and evaluation than other services but rather to illustrate the approach to be followed when considering any and all library needs and agency services.

ONLINE ORDERING

Consider the apparently simple statement: "The vendor shall provide online ordering at no additional cost to the library." This is not unreasonable. Capabilities that can be categorized as online ordering are offered by a number of North American subscription agencies, and they are frequently provided as part of the service

BEWARE OF:

—Mismatched expectations
—Mismatched hardware/software interface
—scheduling misunderstandings

package covered by the agency's basic fee. A vendor replies positively, the library contracts for service, and then the problems of definition and mismatched expectations emerge. The vendor provides access to its automated system allowing the library to enter orders online. There is no charge for accessing the order function, but system access is billed at $250 a year plus telecommunications charges, and while the serials department has access to a personal computer, it is not configured with a modem and telecommunications software. Another library enters orders into its local serials control system. The system has the hardware and software to support connection to the agency's system, but there is as yet no interface that will allow orders from the serials control system to be transferred to the agency system. In another situation, an agency provides the service described in the library's stated requirements, but the service does not accomplish the unstated objective that the library assumed would be facilitated by online ordering—the rapid placement of new orders with publishers. Library staff enter orders online into the vendor's system on a daily basis, but the orders are processed only once a week, and are dispatched less frequently.

AGENCY INFORMATION FILES

Agencies' promotional literature often stresses the size of publisher and title files. The implication is that large information files are equivalent to comprehensive coverage of serials materials and superior agency performance. This may be the case, but the significance of file size will vary from library to library.

Large publisher, title, and pricing information files can be impressive. To find out whether these files are meaningful, libraries must ask some questions. Are the records unique, or do the files contain multiple entries for the same titles in different editions or different delivery packages? How many of the records are active, being used to service current orders? It is unusual for a large agency to handle orders for more than 75,000 titles, yet several boast title files of 200,000 records. Most libraries subscribe to relatively common titles and rarely make extensive changes in their lists. Libraries with special interests or known trouble spots should assess vendors' files on the basis of their coverage of the materials of concern—medical or financial titles, Spanish serials published in the United States, South East Asian imprints, Latin American newspapers, journals from Eastern Europe, non-periodical serials from publishers that other suppliers have had difficulty handling, etc.

QUESTIONS TO ASK:

—How extensive are the files?
—Are records unique, or duplicated?
—How current is the information?
—Are special interests matched?
  Technical titles? Foreign titles?
—How convenient is access?

An agency must have accurate and up-to-date information on titles, publishers, and subscription rates. Accuracy and timeliness are the relevant issues, not the size of the files or the format in which they are maintained. In libraries other than corporate libraries, subscription lists are relatively static, undergoing less than five percent change per annum. Most libraries have only a limited need to access the information in an agency's publisher and title files. When such a need does arise, it can be satisfied from a variety of sources; subscription agency files are only one option. Increased competition among the publishers of periodical and serials directories has improved the general availability, quality, and timeliness of bibliographic and publisher data. As a result, variations in the quality of the publisher and title files of competing subscription agencies appear to have decreased.

If an agency's files offer an acceptable and cost-effective way of meeting a library's needs, then convenience of access becomes an issue. Are the following options available: a quick phone call on a toll-free line, a printed catalog of high demand titles, specialist catalogs tailored to the needs of different types of libraries, or online access to the agency's files? No one method will be available, appropriate, or superior in all situations and, in some cases, online access to a large file of agency data *may* be the best solution to a library's service needs.

CLAIMING SUPPORT

Agency support for claiming is generally considered to be a valuable service for libraries. It can be, provided a library has thought through its requirements and assessed how agency services address those requirements. The following discussion focuses on claiming missing issues of active periodical subscriptions; different lines of inquiry would be needed to assess agency support for claiming non-periodical serials, claims arising from problems in the placement or timing of new orders or subscription renewals, duplicates, and the replacement of damaged or defective material.

Having determined existing patterns of issue non-receipt and the results of claiming during the profiling of the collection, the next steps are to examine the environment in which the library operates and the claiming support services provided by vendors.

It can be instructive to ask agencies what statistics they maintain on their claiming activities as a means of comparison with what the library knows about its own claiming patterns, or as an indication of the potential relevance of different services. In the early 1970s, 74 percent of claims handled by one large U.S. agency were for single missing issues, 15 percent arose from the interruption of subscriptions at renewal time, 2 percent were due to publication delays, 1.5 percent involved problems with multiple copy orders, and 1 percent was for indexes or supplements not known to the agency. Between 2 and 7.5 percent of the items claimed generated second or subsequent claims.[89]

Items become eligible for claiming when a library recognizes that one or more issues of a title have not been received. Non-receipt of issues against an active subscription can be caused by a number of factors, including inaccurate prediction of the expected date of receipt of an issue, publication delays, losses in transit to the library, losses between receipt in the library and check-in, and inaccurate check-in.

Claiming cannot be initiated until library staff become aware that an item is missing. In libraries with manual serials control systems, comprehensive identification of missing issues requires regular review of all active check-in records. In situations where records for both active and inactive serials are maintained in a single sequence, this means regular review of all serials records. Depending on the titles in a collection, "regular" may also mean frequent since a number of publishers will not honor claims for material more than three months after issue, and others maintain only limited quantities of back-stock which are distributed on a first-claimed first-served basis.

In manual systems, the number of records to be inspected can be reduced by maintaining separate files for active and inactive titles, placing new orders in a holding file until receipt of the first issue, or color-coding records for titles with different frequencies and establishing different schedules for review of the weekly, monthly, and quarterly titles thus identified. If such procedures can be implemented without disrupting service to users, they can simplify record review. However, comprehensive gap identification remains a time-consuming and labor intensive process.

Some automated serials systems offer relief from the workload of missing issue identification. The nature and extent of automatic gap recognition support varies from system to system. Some systems merely allow an item to be flagged for claiming when an operator recognizes that an issue is missing. Others support operator review of check-in records for all titles of a given frequency or alert the operator when the check-in of a current issue causes a gap in the expected sequence, for example, signalling the gap created by the check-in of a July issue on a screen that accommodates the check-in of one item per month when no receipt has been recorded for June. Alternatively, a system may select all records with no check-in activity in a given time period and present these for review. More sophisticated systems allow the definition of complex prediction algorithms for each title and automatically generate claim alerts when the pattern of receipt varies from the pattern that it has been profiled to expect.

If a library lacks the staff or systems to identify gaps in receipt on a regular basis, it should determine how the gaps that are recognized are discovered; possible recognition points include unsatisfied user requests, annual review of records by students during summer vacation, or assembly of issues for binding. The library should decide what action is taken when gaps are noticed. Does the library claim only missing issues of expensive titles or those scheduled for binding? Are there patterns in publishers' responses to the claims that the library does generate such as: consistent non-availability because of delays in claiming or routine requests for proof of payment because the claims are for expensive materials? Can the library really use a vendor's claim support services, or would it be more appropriate to look for support in purchasing single issue back copies? If a vendor has a missing copy bank or special arrangements with a back issue dealer, do these services cover the titles the library claims?

Once a gap has been identified by manual or automated methods, library staff decide whether a claim should be issued. Responsible claiming requires that the receipt record be reviewed before a claim is issued. Unnecessary claims are expensive for libraries, for subscription agencies, and for publishers. [In 1974, 18 percent of the work of one large agency related to claims, and observers estimate that claims account for 8 to 10 percent of some publishers' circulation work.[90]] The review evaluates the legitimacy of a proposed claim based on the formal publication pattern of the title (for example, monthly 11 times a year with no August issue) and the less formal patterns of past receipt (for example, monthly but the issue bearing the name of a given month is always received two months after the cover date). With most periodical serials, it is reasonable to assume that a claim is valid if the issue following a missing issue has been received.

The informed human review of claims is as essential in automated systems as in manual systems, and is of equal importance for claims sent direct to publishers as for those routed through subscription agencies. Automated systems which generate claims quickly and easily increase the number of claims received by serials vendors. Some vendors assign additional staff to handle these claims, only to find that many of the claims are not legitimate. Other agencies may choose not to review the claims, forwarding them direct to publishers without review. A high incidence of invalid claims may result in publishers being less responsive to all claims from all sources.[91]

What constitutes appropriate action when a claim is warranted? Will library users be content to wait 45 to 60 days[92] for the resolution of a claim through an agency, or is more urgent action required? What statistics are available on the speed of publisher responses to claims forwarded direct to the publisher by the library? Are there significant differences in requirements and responsiveness for domestic and foreign titles? In most instances, claims to domestic publishers receive a faster response when submitted direct to publishers. The situation is less clear-cut in relation to foreign publications; agency support may be more valuable for these materials. Are the response requirements different for different parts of the collection? If a faster response is essential, what is an acceptable time frame? Does the library have resources such as staff or an automated system to generate claims, access to a reliable file of publisher names and addresses, and the budget allocation to cover postage, phone or fax charges to relay the claims to publisher so that it can claim direct from publishers and rely on vendor support only in those cases where a publisher demands proof of payment before responding to a claim? The importance of speed in claiming may be influenced by factors other than user expectations. Some publishers maintain only a limited number of replacement copies. In addition, a library's chance of obtaining a replacement issue may be adversely affected by submitting claims through an agency because of delays in dealing through a third party (and the probability that an agency will dispatch multiple claims from multiple libraries at the same time).

Standard agency claim support does not extend to assistance in identifying gaps in the receipt of issues. However, some vendors offer services that can be helpful in determining the validity of proposed claims when gaps have been identified by the library: printed or online reports of publication schedules, irregularities, and delays submitted by participating publishers. The relevance of such services will depend upon the proportion of a library's titles covered, the number of claims caused by publication delays, the availability of library staff to check potential claims against the reporting service, the ease of accessing the service, and the nature of any charges for the service. [At least one U.S. vendor offers a centralized online check-in service which provides users with access to the records of other libraries to determine whether they have recorded receipt of an item for which a claim is being considered. Similar capabilities are available to any library with access to the check-in records of other institutions. Again, the utility of such files depends on coverage, the availability of staff to check the records, and the costs of accessing the files.]

If a formal claim is deemed appropriate, it must be prepared and dispatched. Procedures differ for libraries claiming through subscription agencies and those claiming direct from publishers. All claims must include title, identification of the issue being claimed, and the name and address of the library. A library claiming direct must also determine the publisher's name and the address to which claims are to be sent. It may also need to provide order details. When a library places its claims through an agent, the agency supplies publisher names and addresses and order and payment details. In some libraries these services will have significant value, while in others they will not. The determining factors include the number of publishers to which a library submits claims, the stability of these publishers' addresses, and the proportion of a library's claims for which publishers request order and payment verification.

Agency claim services may entail hidden costs. For instance, a vendor may require that claims be submitted on a standard claim form using the vendor form of title, title number, invoice number, etc. If the vendor's form of title differs from that used by the library, additional effort will be required to access and transcribe the vendor's form of title. Will the vendor accept claims printed from the library's automated serials control system? Can the agency provide an interface for the electronic transmission of claims from the local serials system, or must claims be printed and forwarded by mail? Who bears the costs of interface development and the communications charges for electronic transmission?

Simply because a vendor offers an automated claim service does not necessarily mean that the service will reduce library workloads, save money, or speed claiming. Each situation must be assessed on its merits. This requires careful thought and probing questioning. It's all too easy to assume that automated means "better" or "faster" or "less expensive." Every assumption must be identified and tested. A library with manual systems may feel that it is desirable to use an agent that supports online entry of claims. The accuracy of this judgement depends on what benefits the library expects to receive from the system and whether or not the system provides them. If speed is an issue, online entry of claims will almost certainly move them from the library to the agency more rapidly than the postal service. (Fax will do the same.) Library use of these technologies will not *necessarily* contribute to more speedy dispatch of claims from agency to publisher. Claims entered online by a library may not be input directly into an agency's claim generation system. In some cases, reports received electronically are printed and rekeyed into the claim system. What is the agency's schedule for the generation *and* dispatch of claims to publishers? Although an agency may enter claims into the computer on a daily basis, it may process them only once a week and dispatch them even less frequently. It is also worth noting that entering claims daily does not necessarily mean that claims are entered on the day they are received.

An agency may delay the dispatch of claims (or orders) to a publisher until a critical mass of transactions has been accumulated. Agencies realize obvious benefits from batching claim processing and dispatching multiple claims to publishers at one time. What is the effect on a library? How do publishers respond to the bulk receipt of multiple claims?

Although the electronic transmission of claims to publishers appears to have obvious benefits for libraries, this is not always the case. The majority of publishers cannot accept electronic claims. The service will be relevant only for libraries with significant numbers of orders with the publishers serviced *and* a recurring need to claim items from these publishers. If these conditions prevail, other issues must be considered. What is the nature of an agent's electronic communication with publishers? Is the transfer accomplished using fax, an electronic mail system, an online connection between the agency's system and the publisher's automated system, or the monthly dispatch of magnetic tapes? Does the use of an agency's automated services entail additional costs for the library for use of the service, for equipment, or for data transmission? Can the vendor demonstrate time savings and improved response rates through the use of such systems?

A library that is serious about claiming retains a record of claims issued and monitors claim responses, dispatching second and subsequent claims as necessary. Publishers' responses to claims range from no apparent action, through communication explaining publication irregularities or requesting proof that the library has a valid order for the title, to dispatch of the missing issue. Each type of response requires an appropriate adjustment to the file of claim records and, if replacement material is not received, provision of proof of payment or issuance of a second and, possibly, a third claim.

Subscription agencies routinely provide claim tracking support. The usual approach is to issue printed reports at library-specified intervals listing the claims submitted through the agency and the

—Does the agency have statistics on its claiming activities?

—How are gaps identified? Manually? Automatically?

—Can the vendor supply missing copies?

—How long does it take?

—How important is speed?

—How is agency performance monitored?

responses the agency has received from publishers. Such reports relieve the library of the need to maintain records of the claims submitted through an agency. The reports serve as a check-list of potentially outstanding claims. After determining that the items for which no responses are shown have not subsequently been received, the library returns the marked-up list to the agency, which then issues further claims as appropriate.

This service is usually provided free of charge. But if the library has special needs, can these be accommodated? For instance, does the listing use the library's form of title or the agency's form of title? Is there a significant difference between the two for titles claimed frequently? Difficulties with title interpretation can be a cause of frequent claims if inexperienced library staff are unable to locate the appropriate check-in record for items with multiple or confusing titles. Does the library need a single claims report for all subscriptions, or would it be better served by separate reports for each ship to address?

After profiling the pattern of missing issues and claiming activity in the library and reviewing library needs against the range of available agency services, library staff must determine whether agency support for claiming is appropriate and, if so, which range of services is most relevant. Such an examination may also uncover areas where routine procedures would be inappropriate, for example, sections of the collection for which speed of claiming is of paramount importance, or titles for which claiming is unproductive and should be replaced by back issue purchase.

If the analysis reveals that for the library in question, some elements of vendor claim support would be valuable, the next step is to prepare statements of service requirements and performance objectives. Such statements should not only reflect the needs of the library but they should also reflect the realities of the claiming process:

> . . . libraries can expect the same treatment of a claim through their agent as they would receive if they had ordered directly from the publisher. . . . a library does not purchase any special treatment flowing from the agency-publisher business relationship.[93]

The library's objectives must be realistic and informed by discussion with other libraries and agencies. There is no point in defining "acceptable" levels for missing issue claims arising from factors other than late renewal of orders. An agency has no control over the factors that cause these missing issues, and can do little directly to influence publishers' responses to these claims other than providing as much detail as possible about the order from which the claim originates to validate the library's eligibility for a replacement issue. For these materials, a library can expect to receive positive responses to requests for the following services from an agency: assistance in the validation of potential claims, support for the preparation of machine-readable claims and their electronic transmission to the agency, publisher name and address data, payment verification when required, dispatch of claims to the publisher within specified time limits, claim tracking reports at library specified schedules, preparation of second and subsequent claims upon receipt of marked-up claim report listings from the library, and the statistics of claim activity on the library's account.

Statements of service requirements should include mechanisms for monitoring agency performance. For some services, agency performance can only be evaluated by whether or not the agency provides (and continues to provide) the service sought by the library in the form specified or in an alternative form that is acceptable to the library and within the negotiated cost parameters. For others, more precise performance criteria can be defined. For example, a library might require that a vendor be capable of supporting the electronic transmission of machine-readable claims output from serials control system X and that the vendor provide a toll-free line for transmission of this data. In most circumstances, there will be neither the need nor opportunity for defining performance criteria for this capability. On the other hand, after discussion with several agencies, a library might reasonably require that an agency provide toll-free facsimile lines for receipt of claims and that, except when agency procedures reveal that a claim is unnecessary, the agency dispatch all claims to publishers within two working days of receipt of the claim.

Analysis may reveal that traditional vendor support for claiming is not appropriate and that the library would be better served by foregoing that support in favor of online access to a vendor's publisher name and address file. In this case, the availability, quality, and cost of accessing such files becomes a higher priority than traditional claiming support services, the non-use of which can become a focus for the negotiation of lower service fees for agency management of the library's account. In another library, the only claim support required from a vendor may be the generation of a listing of the addresses of all publishers from which the library orders material. In other situations, agency claim support may be rendered superfluous by the library's purchase of a directory of periodical publishers.

COMMUNICATING REQUIREMENTS

Once it has defined its requirements, a library must then communicate them to potential vendors. The formality of the process will vary. At the simplest level, a serials manager might use a page of handwritten notes as a reminder when calling vendors to inquire about their interest in submitting quotes for service, surveying suppliers at a library show, or discussing vendor capabilities with colleagues. If a library has specific requirements that *must* be met by any vendor wishing to service its account, it will save time for the library and vendors if these are spelled out in a written letter or memo. [Written communication is also the most appropriate way for a library to signal its serious concern or dissatisfaction with the service it receives from a vendor.] The most formal procedures are followed by libraries required to obtain competitive bids for serial subscription services. In these circumstances, a formal bid document or request for proposal will be prepared requiring a response in a defined format to be submitted by a specific date. Formal bid situations are most common among state institutions (one estimate suggests that as many as 75 percent of public libraries and 63 percent of schools are required to bid)[94] and government agencies. Bidding is less common among academic libraries, but some administrations are beginning to require that libraries seek competitive bids in an attempt to cut serial costs.[95]

BID SPECIFICATIONS

Many librarians dislike formal bid procedures for the supply of serials:

> Librarians generally believe that bidding hampers the freedom and efficiency of the acquisitions process. The bidding process is labor-intensive because of the difficulty of writing good bid specifications. It is also troublesome because of the concern about disruption of service and the difficulty of documenting value added by agents who emphasize service

and good business practices. Many librarians question if there are any benefits, because the general consensus is that the costs saved by procuring the lowest bidder are lost by costs incurred in the bidding process.[96]

Agencies also dislike bidding. It is expensive to prepare bid responses, many bids are awarded on the basis of cost with little regard to quality of service, and it is costly for an agency to establish service on an account previously handled by another agency. In many bid situations, the award is for a relatively short period—one to two years. This gives an agency little chance to recover start-up costs. Furthermore, there is no guarantee that good service will be rewarded by renewal of the contract.

Although many of these concerns are valid, the discipline a formal bid situation imposes by mandating that a library document its requirements and selection criteria is a valuable communication tool that can facilitate smooth serials acquisitions.

A library required to seek formal bids must develop its request for bids within the constraints of the guidelines of its governing authority or parent institution. In situations where there is some flexibility, the following suggestions can be of assistance to libraries seeking to obtain the widest range of competitive responses:

Accommodate Multiple Vendors: If a collection contains distinct groups of materials with different pricing and service characteristics, use a bid format that will allow awards to multiple vendors. This approach is beneficial when a collection contains popular magazines, domestic and foreign periodicals, and/or periodical and non-periodical serials. Among periodicals, the popular and domestic/foreign distinctions may have a positive impact on pricing, thus enabling the library to obtain a more attractive proposal from different vendors than from a single vendor. The periodical/non-periodical distinction may allow a library to take advantage of the higher discounts for non-periodical serials often provided by book vendors and can also be beneficial in providing service options that mirror the different acquisitions characteristics of these materials. A document that allows awards to multiple vendors need not necessarily result in the choice of multiple vendors, since one vendor may be the most satisfactory service provider in all categories.

Define Award Procedures: When preparing a specification that allows multiple-vendor awards, describe how such awards will be made. Vendors are more likely to respond, and to respond with favorable terms, when all materials in a defined class are to be awarded to a single vendor. Vendors are wary of undefined multiple vendor bids since some libraries use them to pick the best from each vendor's response, placing orders with multiple vendors but ordering from each only those titles the vendor offers at a discount from list price and/or those with no service charge.

Critically Evaluate Bid Specifications from Other Libraries: Many librarians who are prepared to research their local serials acquisitions environments and needs do not maintain their vigilance when documenting these requirements in a formal bid specification. It can be helpful to review sample specifications from other libraries or from vendors, but they should not be adopted without careful thought.

Guard Against Unintentional Disqualification of Vendors: Libraries are justifiably anxious to ensure that bidders have the capabilities and experience to provide reliable service. They seek to qualify bidders by defining basic levels of corporate capability and service provision that must be met for a vendor to secure an award. In a competitive situation, the objective of such qualification is to identify and weed out unreliable or incompetent vendors, not to reduce the number of eligible vendors to only one or two companies. Vendor qualification elements should be developed against an awareness of the structures and services common to most vendors.

A requirement that a bidder provide the names of three current clients with collections of similar size and scope to that of the library seeking bids is not unduly restrictive. Nor, in most cases, is the further requirement that these libraries be in the same state or region as the library issuing the bid request. And, of course, contract award will depend upon the named libraries supplying satisfactory reports on the vendor. On the other hand, a requirement that a bidder have an organizational structure that includes regional and/or international offices would disqualify a number of reputable agencies as would a requirement that all orders be cleared direct with publishers rather than through another agency or the representative of another agency. If a library is concerned about these aspects of agency service, it is more rewarding to include specifications that address the specifics of these concerns directly. For example, the library may request that the vendor indicate the hours during which vendor personnel are available for consultation by library staff, detail the services and procedures used to offset communication restrictions imposed by distance, detail any classes of material that the bidder acquires through other agencies or their representatives rather than direct from publishers, and indicate the benefits that accrue to the library from such supply arrangements.

Proscriptive description of service requirements can also limit the number of vendors eligible to respond and the competitiveness of the bids received. Few agencies offer missing issue banks. While this may be a service that a library considers essential, its inclusion as a mandatory requirement may mean that a library receives only one qualified bid. A sole qualified vendor is unlikely to offer service at a price as competitive as it would bid were it in competition with other vendors. A requirement that a vendor be able to provide an automated serials check-in system in addition to serials acquisition services will also limit the number of responses a library can expect to receive when it issues a request for bid. A library may well decide that provision of a special service not widely supported by serials subscription agencies is essential to its operations. In doing so, it should recognize the likely consequence of a limited number of acceptable responses and the possible impact of such limitation on pricing.

Spell Out Any Special Requirements: A bid request document is a communications tool. In their responses, potential service providers communicate their understanding of the library's requirements in dollar terms. In closed bid situations, these documents represent the only allowable communication between the parties during the bid process. It is the library's responsibility to obtain the best service at the most competitive price. A bid specification which fails to mention any unusual service requirements may result in a lower bid price; it is also likely to result in service that does not meet the library's special needs. Conversely, a library that makes minimal use of a standard service but fails to mention that fact will probably receive good service but at a price higher than it needs to pay.

PRICE QUOTES

In both formal bid situations and less formal inquiries, libraries frequently request that potential vendors provide individual price quotations for each title in the collection. On the surface, this appears to be a reasonable request: the library supplies a list of all current titles, vendors submit their quotes, the quotes from different vendors are compared, and the supply contract is awarded to the vendor quoting the lowest price. However, this approach is flawed. As detailed in the discussion of service charges, it is time-consuming, costly, and unrewarding for an agency to check its price files for each title submitted by a prospective client. It is also time-consuming and frustrating for libraries to interpret and compare quotes from different vendors.

For domestic periodicals, all vendors attempt to quote the same prices—the publisher's list price for the subscription year for which the quote is requested. Variations are not uncommon when two or more vendors are asked to submit title-by-title quotes for the same periodicals for the same time period. If these quotes are compared with the library's existing documentation on the cost of obtaining the titles from its current vendor, even more variations will appear. The prices quoted by different vendors can vary for a number of reasons including:

- the timeliness with which agencies record publisher price updates (the more timely the files, the higher the prices quoted)
- the ability of agency systems to access pricing data for multiple subscription periods (the current subscription year and the next subscription year, for example)
- confusion over the period for which the quote is requested (the current subscription year or the next subscription year), and
- and differences in vendor interpretation of library requirements(regular subscription price or membership price, edition or format required, preferred method of delivery, and the type of coverage sought, for example, a basic subscription or a full subscription including indexes).

The potential for variation is greater when comparing quotes for foreign periodicals and non-periodical serials. For foreign publications, the direct variables expand to include different agency practices for calculating exchange rates—the rate at the time the quote is prepared, the agency's prediction for the rate of exchange at the time the subscription will be placed, and an agency's decision as to whether to use official exchange rates or the internal rates offered by some major foreign publishers. For non-periodical serials, the areas for misinterpretation widen to encompass the effect of publication schedules and delays. Does a quote for the 1991 subscription year include the issues scheduled for publication for 1990 that are delayed as well as the issues scheduled for publication in 1991, and how does an agency interpret a library's request for a calendar year quote when the publisher quotes prices on a volume basis?

Only a library has the incentive to resolve such differences. Agencies that will agree to absorb variations from quoted prices for a specified additional service charge are selective in the titles for which they offer such service. In all other circumstances, it is standard practice for agencies to pass on to libraries any and all additional charges arising from price increases and costs for materials or services not covered in the initial quote. In situations in which price is a significant element in vendor selection, there is an incentive for vendors to choose the lowest cost interpretation in uncertain areas, and vendors who are tardy in updating their price files may enjoy an advantage over competitors who quote more up-to-date prices.

Title-by-title price quotations can cause confusion and may also fail to reveal all elements of the pricing structure used by an agency. Depending on the wording of a request for a price quotation, an agency may be fully responsive without revealing important details of its service charges and special charges for certain categories of materials.

It can be more informative for a library to use a pricing-by-category approach. Provide vendors with a full list of the titles for which service is required. Divide the list into consumer magazines, U.S. periodicals, foreign periodicals, U.S. non-periodical serials, and foreign non-periodical serials. For each category, request that each vendor:

- identify titles it cannot handle and give reasons why this material cannot be serviced.
- identify titles for which the invoiced subscription price will be lower than the publisher's subscription price, specifying the minimum discount guaranteed for these titles for the upcoming subscription period.
- identify titles for which the subscription price invoiced will be higher than the publisher's list price, specifying all circumstances in which additional charges are applied and the level of each charge.
- identify any other circumstances in which the subscription price invoiced may vary from the publisher's list price.
- specify the service charge that will apply to these materials, expressing the charge as a percentage of the publishers' list price.
- identify any circumstances under which the stated service charge will vary, providing examples of the titles affected by such variations.
- detail any additional charges that will apply to the provision of basic subscription service.

Additionally, for non-U.S. materials:

- detail the approach to currency conversion, the application of charges for foreign exchange transactions, and any additional charges that are applied to the handling of non-U.S. publications.
- provide subscription price quotations and statements of all applicable service charges for a library-selected sample of fifteen titles for a library-specified subscription period—the current subscription year or next subscription year. The titles specified for quotation should include ten of the most expensive titles on the library's list and another five titles representative of the foreign materials in its collection.

And, for non-periodical serials also:

- identify any additional charges for management of these titles.
- identify titles that the publisher ships to the vendor and detail the charges levied for handling and re-shipping these materials.
- provide subscription price quotations, statements of all applicable service charges, *and* copies of the vendor's standard reports on current publication status for a library-selected sample of fifteen titles for a library-specified subscription period.

In addition to providing a more complete and accurate picture of an individual vendor's prices and charging policies, this approach also allows libraries to discern clearly differences among different vendors' treatment of different types of materials. In many instances, such segmentation of a library's list can provide opportunities for more favorable pricing, especially if the library is in a position to divide servicing of its account among multiple vendors.

VENDOR SELECTION AND NEGOTIATION

Libraries that have committed the time and resources to:

- surveying the services and pricing practices of a range of vendors,
- clearly and critically assessing the specifics of local needs for serials acquisition support,
- discussing the performance of competing vendors with other libraries with similar serials collections and needs,

- defining and prioritizing vendor selection criteria, and
- soliciting formal or informal service and pricing proposals from a range of potential service providers

may find the actual process of vendor selection something of an anticlimax.

Library investigations and vendor responses will reveal the subset of potential vendors that can meet a library's minimum service requirements and indicate the cost parameters within which such services are available. Once this subset has been determined, the application of local needs and priorities will facilitate further deselection on price, service, and/or reputation. If the results suggest that no vendor is qualified to meet the library's requirements, the library should reexamine and adjust its decisions on needs and priorities. If one or more vendors appear qualified, negotiation is the appropriate response.

The selection and negotiation approach should not be abandoned if only one vendor appears responsive to a library's requirements. Even in closed bid situations, many libraries have the opportunity to fine-tune their agreements with the selected vendor(s), at least in regard to details of how services will be implemented.

Nor should information gathering be suspended during vendor assessment. The primary objective is to identify the vendor(s) offering service and pricing packages that appear to meet best the library's needs and priorities. However, the process also entails flagging issues for query and clarification and developing a list of negotiating topics. The proposal of a vendor deemed non-responsive on matters of high priority may still contain service or pricing approaches that can provide useful points for discussing with a more responsive vendor selected for negotiation.

NEGOTIATION

Negotiation has two objectives: to reach the best possible service and pricing agreement and to clarify service requirements and commitments. A negotiation is not an end, but a beginning. Neither party should look to emerge as *the* victor. The aim is for *both* parties to win by laying a solid foundation for a smooth and mutually beneficial service relationship.

Negotiation proceeds most smoothly when conducted through direct contact between library and vendor. If practical, a face-to-face meeting or telephone conference is more satisfactory than correspondence. When approaching a vendor to arrange a formal discussion session, a library should indicate that it wishes to clarify details of service and pricing and to establish mutually acceptable procedures and criteria for monitoring service provision. Reference should be made to any specific points the library wishes to clarify or negotiate, and the vendor should be asked to provide a representative authorized to make binding commitments on its behalf. In most situations (including multi-vendor bid situations), a library should also indicate that the negotiation is part of its vendor selection process and that an invitation to negotiate does not indicate that the vendor has been selected as *the* service provider.

In preparation for negotiation, library personnel should review their requirements and give some thought to the likely responses of agencies. For most libraries, the focus will be on service adjustments, pricing packages, and the definition of mutually acceptable performance evaluation criteria and penalties for non-performance. Vendors are likely to be interested in strategies that increase their revenues and/or reduce their expenses: securing all of a library's business, negotiating a multi-year commitment, defining the services covered by the basic service charge or handling fee, or securing a commitment for additional products and/or services. As performance monitoring and evaluation are more important to a library than they are to an agency, library staff should prepare a range of concrete proposals for discussion.

Prior to negotiation, library managers must also determine their bottom line position by identifying any agreements or concessions that are to be treated as *essential* prerequisites for a satisfactory relationship between the library and its agency. In many instances, there will be no such pivotal issues, but when there are, it is important that the person(s) representing the library have a clear understanding of institutional priorities.

There are no tricks of the trade that will ensure a successful negotiation. The most important thing to remember is that the objective is to establish the framework for a solid working relationship: a service and pricing package that *both* parties can live with. At the end of a negotiation, the library representative should document the agreements reached and submit them to the vendor for confirmation on the understanding that the summary of negotiations will be part of any service agreement between the library and the vendor.

The recommended approach—critical and systematic needs definition and prioritization, vendor evaluation, and negotiation of service and pricing packages—works. It can be applied to assist a library in achieving a variety of serials acquisition objectives encompassing both service provision and pricing. Using a formal

RFP process, Utah State University successfully pursued a significant reduction in agency service charges through vendor consolidation:

> The original goal of consolidation was savings in service charges. Our new service charge rate is less than half the composite amount we were previously paying to . . . three separate vendors. Accordingly, in the first year of the change, U.S.U. saved approximately $17,500 in service charges alone. In the years when the university's budget office allows us to prepay, the interest earned through the vendor's prepayment plan could cover our service charge fees at the new rate. As agreed in the RFP response, we are guaranteed this new service charge for three years and the same rate or lower for the following three years.[97]

In the past several years, a number of other academic libraries have achieved substantial savings in service charges through informed negotiation with vendors. The emphasis is necessarily on "informed." There is little to be gained in negotiating for a price break through a lower service fee or gratis service without giving due consideration to other aspects of pricing and service. A low service charge on inflated subscription prices is no bargain! Nor is favorable pricing when services essential to the smooth operations of a library's serials acquisitions are not part of the deal. Finally, negotiation is a two-way street: no vendor wishing to remain viable and in business will give away the store without extracting an appropriate return such as handling all of a library's serial orders or obtaining a multi-year service contract.

USING AN AGENCY

If a library is to obtain maximum benefit from subscription agency services, the serials manager's responsibilities do not end with the negotiation of a service agreement and selection of a vendor. That is only the beginning.

The relationship between a library and an agency is ongoing and lasts for at least one and usually two years or more. It is in the best interests of both parties to work at perfecting the fit between a library's needs and an agency's capabilities within mutually acceptable financial parameters. An agency cannot afford dissatisfied customers; a library cannot afford an unsatisfactory relationship with its supplier. The universe of agencies capable of meeting the needs of a specific library is not so large that a library can summarily abandon one agency and move on to another. This might work for a while but if a library's only response to service deficiencies is to change agencies, it will soon work its way through all the viable options and be back where it started.

It is rare for an agency's initial service implementation to achieve a perfect fit with a library's needs. And, both libraries and vendors operate in a fluid, changing environment. Over time, vendors' services and procedures change as do libraries' needs and priorities. For the relationship to be successful, both parties must recognize and accommodate these realities. Neither agency personnel nor library staff can read minds. A library can no more intuit changes in agency procedures than an agency can reach a telepathic understanding of a library's dissatisfaction with its performance. Communication is essential if both parties are to get what they need from the relationship.

This chapter discusses the working relationship between libraries and agencies. It explores the chemistry of library- agency relationships, common causes of library dissatisfaction with agencies, methods for monitoring agency performance, and procedures for addressing service deficiencies and changing vendors.

COMMUNICATION

In return for savings in operating costs, a library that uses vendors for serials acquisition relinquishes a certain degree of flexibility and the freedom to rely on informal communication and ad hoc procedures. The significance of these changes is not always anticipated. No matter how responsive an agency is, a library will experience annoying delays in communication and some surrender of responsiveness and control.

For example, when a library places an order direct with a publisher, it is relatively easy to confirm that the order has been sent by checking the on-order file, by looking up the records of checks cut for the department, or by simply asking the order clerk whether the order has been dispatched. Similarly, if some weeks elapse and the library has received neither a response from the publisher nor any issues of the new title, there are several avenues that can be pursued to confirm that the publisher received the order, including review of cancelled checks and/or a phone call to the publisher. The library can take immediate action to determine the status of the order and implement corrective action. If delays in fulfillment of the order cause concern, there is a varied range of candidates to whom blame can be assigned: the order clerk, the administrative unit responsible for issuing checks, the U.S. Postal Service, and/or the publisher.

The situation is different when a library is tracing an order placed through a subscription agency. Unless the library has online access to an up-to-date file of the orders placed by its vendor, there will be an interval of apparent inactivity before the library can verify that the order reached the agency and was forwarded to the publisher. The period of inactivity may only be brief and apparent rather than actual, spanning the time required for the library to phone or fax the agency and for the agency to access its records, find the relevant information, and relay that information to the library. But, the need to deal through a third party *will* cause frustration. And, if problems are revealed and blame is being assigned, who is the obvious candidate—the order clerk, the U.S. Postal Service, the agency, the U.S. Postal Service (again), or the publisher? Human nature being what it is, the likelihood is that the preferred culprit will be the party that is common to all snafus the library has occasion to investigate—the agency!

Or, when a library uses an agency and the administration requests an urgent analysis of serials expenditures by criteria different from those usually reported, the serials manager cannot readily assess the availability of the data and the resources required to assemble it. Instead of being able to give an immediate response to the request—indicating what data can be provided, in what time-frame, and at what cost in terms of the effect of pulling staff from other duties to prepare the report—the manager must contact the library's agency (or agencies) and determine the type(s) of data available and the period(s) of delay before the data is in hand. Agency responses may seem less than cooperative: the agency does not support access to the requested data; information cannot be provided on supplemental charges and credits; the data can be prepared but only as part of the routine report run next Tuesday week; the library excluded financial report generation when negotiating for reduced service charges, so an extra charge will accrue; or, if speed is critical, there will be an additional charge for express delivery. After all that, the manager then has to go back to the administrator to redefine the report and announce a time-frame that appears to be less than responsive. This is an extreme example; most agencies are responsive to such requests, and few address the issue of additional charges for extraordinary services with any vigor. What it does illustrate is that without careful forethought, the use of vendors can cause feelings of diminished control among library personnel and anxiety about how administrators and users will react to the apparent non-responsiveness of library services.

Failure to recognize and plan for the buffering effects of vendors on a library's communication and response channels is a major cause of library dissatisfaction with agency services. At the simplest level, appropriate planning requires recognition and formalization of communications procedures previously handled by casually asking a colleague: "When you checked with publisher X last week, they did say that it was the annual reviews that were running behind, not the yearbooks, didn't they?" It also requires analysis of communication priorities that were previously within the direct and immediate control of the library: expectations about publisher responsiveness to new orders, the amount of time that should elapse between claims, etc. and definition of exceptional conditions—the circumstances in which standard routines should be abandoned in favor of special action.

The effective use of agency services requires that a library develop procedures to support interaction with its vendor(s). The functions to be accommodated include: negotiating performance criteria and procedures for problem resolution, monitoring agency performance and library needs, formulating and/or adjusting service requirements and expectations, and communicating service requirements. The critical factor is recognition of the need for formalized communication. Rather than preparing written documents with titles like "Standards and Procedures for Library-Agency Communications," serials managers might be better served by placing the following notice in a visible location:

SUBSCRIPTION AGENTS ARE
NOT MIND READERS!

Causes of Library Dissatisfaction: In a survey of 850 libraries of all types and sizes conducted in the early 1970s, Katz and Gellatly found that:

> The single most frequent complaint librarians bring against agents is the lack of meaningful communication in the encounters they have with one another. This non-communication takes many forms: the agent's apparent lack of interest in the library and its problems; the agent's failure to answer letters promptly; the agent's failure to acknowledge claims; the agent's failure to explain his other charges clearly; the agent's failure to . . . well, generally communicate with the librarian in a meaningful and useful way.[98]

Things haven't improved with the passage of time. In a survey of major research libraries in 1985, Derthick and Moran asked participants to list the reasons for their dissatisfaction with serial agents.

> The most common reply was unresponsiveness or slow response to new orders, claims, renewals, and correspondence concerning address changes, adjustments to orders and invoices, multiple subscriptions, cancellations, etc.[99]

In addition, more specific complaints about "poor agent/library relationships" rated the third most frequent mention:

> Respondents believed that the rapid growth of some agents and the transition to automation have caused a deterioration in personalized attention. . . . Others complained of the "erratic quality of customer service staff" or the failure to provide a local representative. Another common criticism of agents was the agents' "failure to deliver advertised services"; "Big promises—of any kind—that are not kept"; "Unfilled promises re: services."[100]

Such comments emphasize the impact of communication on library perceptions of vendor service. They also reveal as much about the unstated service expectations of librarians as they do about deficiencies in vendors' services, suggesting that librarians expect basic agency services to include:

- "interest" in the library and its problems,
- prompt (formal?) replies to correspondence, including correspondence relating to address changes, adjustments to orders and invoices, multiple subscriptions, and cancellations,
- (prompt?) formal acknowledgement of claims,
- full (unprompted?) disclosure of charges,
- rapid (formal?) acknowledgement of new orders and renewals,
- "personalized attention,"
- consistent (high quality?) customer service,
- provision of a local service representative whose duties include visiting the library (once a month?) or phoning the library (once a week?), and
- (voluntary, unprompted?) fulfillment of all service commitments.

Most agencies provide formal acknowledgement of orders and claims. The appearance of these items in a listing of common complaints suggests that there may be a mismatch in expectations as to the form and timeliness of such acknowledgement.

What of the other items? It can be instructive to try to translate these expectations into realistic and measurable performance requirements, to distinguish which of them might be considered part of an agency's basic services, and to assign an appropriate value to those that might constitute additional services. Experience suggests that few if any libraries would have defined these areas of complaint as formal service requirements during vendor selection, clarified their concerns in pre-service negotiations with vendors, or retained these requirements if informed that meeting them would entail additional expense. Once performance was found to be lacking, what action did the libraries take to define appropriate levels of service, communicate and negotiate these requirements with vendors, and monitor future performance?

Service difficulties cut both ways and adversely affect both libraries and agencies. However, while it is clearly in the general interest of agencies to explore and address the service expectations of clients, the responsibility for ensuring that monies expended on external services realize the maximum return in smooth and efficient library operations lies with the library.

WHOSE JOB IS IT?

Is the librarian or the vendor responsible for:

—determining a library's service requirements?
—formulating them into appropriate performance objectives?
—clarifying areas of ambiguity?
—formalizing and recording the objectives?
—monitoring performance against the objectives?
—signalling inappropriate performance?
—initiating discussions to improve performance?

MONITORING VENDOR PERFORMANCE

Ongoing monitoring and evaluation of all aspects of serials acquisitions, including vendor performance, are essential to effective serials management. As with disaster planning, the most effective approach relies on the implementation of a considered plan shaped to accommodate local conditions, rather than an ad hoc response to a sudden emergency. The statements of need, priorities, and vendor selection guidelines developed for initial vendor selection and evaluation highlight the areas of known concern in a specific library situation. The annual review and updating of these guidelines gives staff the opportunity to step back from day-to-day activities to reassess the serials environment, local conditions, and vendor performance, and to identify areas of concern that warrant further study.

If a library is concerned about any aspect of an agency's service or pricing, it is the serial manager's responsibility to define the area of concern, communicate that concern to the agency, and negotiate an appropriate solution. The steps are not dissimilar to those involved in needs definition, vendor selection, and negotiation of the initial service agreement. The atmosphere may be.

DEFINING THE PROBLEM

First, the library must delineate the problem. In some cases, this will be clear cut:

- pricing or service charges which appear to be higher than the agency offers to comparable libraries with similar expenditures, collections, and use of services
- a lower bid for the same titles and services from another vendor
- or the apparent inability of an existing vendor to provide a service considered essential to the library such as machine-readable invoicing data in a format compatible with the library's new automated system or historic pricing data for the titles the library orders through the agency.

In other situations, the dissatisfaction will be less focused and more difficult to quantify:

- high turnover among the agency staff servicing the library's account
- lack of responsiveness to library inquiries and correspondence or
- an apparently high incidence of problems with orders handled by the agency.

It can require considerable effort to define the precise nature of service difficulties before they can be presented for discussion and resolution.

This is not, however, wasted effort. If review and subsequent discussion result in corrective action by the agency, the library has achieved its end. If the agency does not respond adequately to the library's concerns, the analysis will serve as a basis for defining the service requirements to be met by a replacement vendor.

When assessing agency performance against abstract standards or comparing aspects of the performance of different vendors, it is important to make sure that the criteria on which the evaluation is based are actually within the control of the vendor. If a library that splits its orders between two vendors—for example, 500 titles each—experiences a significantly higher claim rate on the materials ordered through vendor A (fifty claims a year) than those obtained through vendor B (fifteen claims a year), it may be tempting to conclude that vendor B provides better service than vendor A. If the uninterrupted receipt of material is important to the library, it could view vendor A's performance as unsatisfactory and request improvement under threat of transferring all orders to vendor B. If vendor A agrees to try to lower claim rates but fails to do so, and the library awards management of all titles to vendor B, it might be surprised when claim rates for the titles previously handled by vendor A actually increase under the management of vendor B. Although there are a number of scenarios under which this could happen, the following is but one example.

The titles managed by vendor A average twelve issues per year and those handled by vendor B average six issues per year; their respective claim rates are one claim per 120 issues and one claim per 200 issues. Claim responses reveal that ten of the fifteen claims on titles handled by vendor B were caused by late renewal of subscriptions. None of the claims for titles handled by vendor A were due to late renewals; all resulted from publication delays or non-receipt of material dispatched by publishers. (Non-receipt was not caused by problems in vendor A's ordering procedures as issues received on all orders had correct names and addresses.) Vendor B maintained its practice of late subscription renewals when it took over management of the titles previously handled by

A, and the claims for these titles increased by 20—10 late renewals with double the impact because of the frequency of publication of these titles. (And vendor A had provided a missing copy bank from which the library had obtained a number of the missing issues that were no longer available from publishers.) A cautionary tale, in which it is also worth noting that had the library assumed direct management of the titles from vendor A, its performance record would not have been any better than that of its ex-vendor.

In this example, a number of issues are hidden within what a library perceived as "a problem with claims." A library manager knowledgeable about the acquisitions characteristics of different types of serials would have realized that it was not appropriate to make direct comparisons of the claim rates for the type of materials handled by vendor A and those managed by vendor B. In exploring the library's concern over claiming, the manager might then have discerned the difference in the types of claims for the titles handled by each vendor and have thus been able to address the issue of late renewals with vendor B and discuss options for more rapid or successful claiming of missing issues of the titles handled by vendor A. In some situations:

> When there is dissatisfaction with one's sole vendor for a class of serials, a group of 100 or so titles can be transferred to another agent, as a test of the service. Or, new orders can be placed with the new agent, and service evaluated in comparison to the original vendor. It must be emphasized, however, that unlike monograph acquisitions, several years may elapse before reliable results can be obtained.[101]

When the dimensions of a problem have been defined, the library's expectations of acceptable service must be expressed in concrete terms so that its requirements can be communicated to the agency. This is also the time to formulate the measures the library proposes to use to monitor agency performance in the problem area. It can be complicated to analyze and translate service requirements, particularly if little thought has been given to the matter prior to the identification of a problem. The issues and approaches are similar to those for defining library needs and priorities.

COMMUNICATING WITH THE AGENCY

Once the library has clarified its concerns and expectations, it is time to communicate those to the agency. This should be done in a formal letter, detailing the problem(s) and stating the action(s) or performance requirement(s) that the library considers would solve the difficulty. The letter, addressed to the agency's chief executive, should seek a time for a formal discussion of the problem and appropriate solutions by vendor representatives and library personnel. Problem resolution can be handled by a meeting or a conference call. [The alacrity and professionalism with which an agency responds to such a request are good indicators of its commitment to service.]

If the literature is an accurate reflection of reality, both librarians and vendors consider that librarians are reluctant and inept when it comes to expressing dissatisfaction and negotiating solutions, and that vendors are skilled at playing on this discomfort. Such a perspective does a disservice to librarians; it depicts them as powerless victims helpless in the hands of master manipulators and suggests that to be successful a serials manager must be critical, suspicious, and aggressive. It also exaggerates the wiles and abilities of the average subscription agency account representative. There may be Machiavellian agency managers who dream of developing highly trained sales representatives skilled in selling exaggerated service promises at inflated prices while putting clients in a hypnotic trance to ensure they never demand delivery of the promised levels of performance. Good luck to them! They will be disappointed.

Subscription agencies are service organizations. Their revenues depend upon delivery of the services their clients expect. While exaggerated promises may attract clients, only proven performance will keep them. It is in the interests of both libraries and agencies to resolve service problems. In problem resolution, the objective should not be to win but to reach an accommodation which meets the needs of both parties: the library's need for trouble-free subscription services and the agency's need for clients.

CHANGING AGENCIES

There is obvious conflict between the published literature and reality on the issue of changing subscription agencies. The literature implies that changing agencies is a painful and disruptive process to be undertaken only as a last resort to save a library from an abysmally incompetent agency. However, in the real world, libraries do change agencies. It is unusual—except in bid situations—for a library to change agencies frequently. However, cost and service competition among vendors and the desire to reduce the number of vendors a library deals with ensure that in any one year, a number of libraries—both large and small—will switch all or part of their serials orders from one vendor to another.

Many librarians view a change in agents as a traumatic process to be avoided at almost any cost:

> Most serial orders are placed with the expectation that the choice of vendor is being made for the long term, an almost permanent commitment.[102]

> Because of multiple and inextricably linked reasons that inhibit changing sources of supply on whim/impulse/sales presentation or even on specific, well-reasoned purpose, the initial selection of source of supply of serials is extremely important.[103]

> Difficulties in changing agents increase with the number of serials involved. No matter what precautions are taken, no matter how cooperative the agents, both old and new, problems are unavoidable.[104]

> For large libraries that have many serial subscriptions placed through one vendor, the overwhelming work in moving several thousand dollars worth of serials titles may keep the serials acquisitions librarian from even contemplating a new vendor. For smaller libraries, a vendor change may be less traumatic but still entail cumbersome paperwork and cause the library to miss some issues.[105]

However, some observers feel that the increasing use of automation in serials operations will facilitate the process of changing vendors:

> There was a time when the last thing an acquisitions librarian wanted to do was change subscription vendors. The cost of revising manual records was a significant disincentive to shopping around. Those days are gone. . . . libraries are now, both technically and psychologically, positioned to make such switches. Vendor-hopping would still entail substantial fulfillment problems and, one can be sure, would not be done capriciously, but it is far more likely today than even five years ago to be a real management option.[106]

Not surprisingly, vendors are relatively silent on the matter. They have an interest in retaining existing customers. Moreover, that interest is served by librarians' anxiety about the disruption caused by a change in supplier. On the other hand, the library market is limited and the subscription business is competitive. The transfer of accounts from one agency to another is a significant source of agency growth. No agency wants to lose a transfer account because a library fears the disruption involved in changing agencies.

Indeed, willy-nilly switching of agencies can place both library and agency in a lose-lose situation. The library experiences disruption, and the agency outlays considerable manpower on implementing the changeover:

> Just as it causes disruptions to a library when agents are changed . . . it causes a great deal of work for the agent to add or drop customers. The rule of thumb in the subscription agency business is that a new account does not really begin to be profitable for the agency until after three years.[107]

It is clearly in the best interests of all parties for a library carefully to consider its options before changing agencies. A library that changes agencies to consolidate orders with fewer agencies has already considered its options and taken them into account in the decision. What are the options for libraries considering a change in vendors as a result of poor service from an agency or an attractive bid from an alternate supplier? First the library should communicate and negotiate with the current supplier.

There will be times when a satisfactory accommodation cannot be reached, when a vendor's performance does not improve, or when a library's decision to change suppliers is based on factors other than problems with the current vendor. No matter what the size of the library or the number of serials to be switched, a change entails extra work for library staff and some disruption in the supply of materials. Planning can eliminate some of the difficulties, but problems should be expected. If a library is switching its orders from one supplier to another, the new agent can be expected to offer a significant level of clerical and system support for the change-over. If such assistance is not volunteered, it should be required as a condition of new vendor selection. Assistance will not be forthcoming if the library is changing from using an agent to ordering direct from publishers.

Wherever possible, a change in supplier should be planned in advance. The library not only needs to establish new channels of supply, it must also deactivate the existing channels.

Deactivation will be relatively routine for periodical subscriptions expiring at the end of the current subscription period. Orders with the current agent are left to run their course and not renewed; renewals are placed with the new agency. To ensure uninterrupted supply, it is essential to verify the expiration dates of current subscriptions. While the records of both the library and its current subscription agency will include expiration dates, these must be verified with the ultimate source of supply—the publishers. It is usual for the agency to which orders are being transferred to undertake such verification by sending inquiry letters to the publishers and tabulating and coordinating responses. The new agency is responsible for placing renewal orders so that there is no lapse in supply. Renewals appear to flow more smoothly if the new agent submits them using the form of library name and address used by the previous agency and annotates the renewal to indicate that the renewal is for an order previously channelled through agency X. If a library has multi-year subscriptions, it can take some time for a full change-over to be effected. Often, the new agent will accept responsibility for processing claims on these titles and acting as the interface for resolving other subscription problems for these materials.

Deactivation is more problematic when dealing with non-periodical serials. The usual procedure is for the library and its new agent to review the receipt status of these materials and request that publishers cancel outstanding orders and replace them with new orders from the new agent. This works relatively smoothly when the initial order has been placed direct with the publisher. The situation becomes more complicated for orders a vendor has placed through an intermediate vendor. A library may receive multiple copies of these materials if the original order has not been cancelled. Planning for a change in vendors should include arrangements for the return of duplicate non-periodical serials and alerts to library staff to check carefully for duplicates before accessioning such items. Few publishers will accept the return of materials that have been stamped or coded with library identification. Vendors that specialize in continuations can assist a library in identifying missing issues or inactive orders by providing checklists of the materials issued by publishers during the period of the change-over. Ultimately, library staff bear the burden of tracing and reactivating lapsed orders.

Any change of suppliers involves substantially amending internal library records, updating supplier information on kardexes, adjusting pricing information, and providing links between the library form of title and that used by the new supplier. [Like libraries, different vendors may use different forms of title for the same publication.] Agencies usually include assistance in updating library records as part of their service offer when seeking to obtain an account that was previously managed by another agent. Such assistance may take the form of the production of customized labels to be affixed to the library's manual records, data entry support or programming to amend records in the library's automated system, and/or provision of agency staff or temporary help to amend manual records.

When changing suppliers, serials managers should request detailed transition plans from the vendors being considered, including references from libraries that have already been through the process. Staff should also investigate the transition assistance received by libraries dealing with other vendors to determine both the range of problems and potential solutions.

The experience of the University of California at Irvine in consolidating orders for 2,800 serials titles with a single vendor suggests that libraries planning a similar change in vendors should:

1. Plan well in advance. A lead time of 1 year should probably be the minimum.
2. Involve . . . staff from the beginning. Be sure that they see the desirability of the project because it will temporarily involve extra work for them. Get their suggestions because their insights will be helpful, and they know better than anyone the impact such an undertaking will have on their procedures and work loads.
3. Develop guidelines so that you have a fixed idea of what you want to do.
4. If possible, begin with an accurate base of information. All the problems of title changes and ceases, duplication and lapses in service will surface in a conversion like this, and must be dealt with. The "cleaner" your records, the easier the conversion.
5. Choose your agent carefully. A good agent will work with you as a partner, offering help and advice throughout the project.
6. After a period of time, evaluate the new agent's performance. . . .[108]

CHEMISTRY, STYLE, OR PERSONA

As in any relationship, an intangible element of style, chemistry, or persona can be a significant factor in library-agency relations. At times, such chemistry appears to be the only explanation for different librarians' radically varying perceptions of the same vendor. Katz and Gellatly found that:

> . . . there was considerable consensus about one agent or another, . . . [however] while 80 percent or more of librarians queried may rank an agent good to excellent, another 20 percent or so may find the same agent only fair to poor. Furthermore, no definite correlation can be established between the size and type of library in the evaluations that are made. The only conclusion arrived at was that the personality—and all that implies—of the librarian and the agent is a dominant factor in satisfactory or unsatisfactory agent-library service.[109]

The importance of this intangible "something" is continually evidenced in the anecdotal literature:

> Reaction to jobbers or dealers is both personal and accidental. Some librarians have excellent results, and others wish they had never run across a particular firm. I know that I have had that result myself. Some dealers have area managers who vary in quality and ability. What may be excellent in California may be inadequate in New York . . . . Other factors may include: change in library staff, promotion, or other separation from dealers, mergers and splits among and within individual jobbers, individual internal library administrations, and the lack of communication of dealer changes.[110]

Finally, there is the *persona* of the serial vending company. This is an intangible element . . . not unlike the impression one receives when interviewing and hiring new staff. What do I know about this company? Is the overall reputation solid? Can I work with the representative? Is the office support for this person dependable? Is the offer the company is making to my library a reasonable one, both for my library and the company? . . . It is not uncommon to find that a vendor may be one library's boon and another's bane. As with any rela-

SAFETY MEASURES

Appropriate safety measures include:

—carefully setting out the library's service requirements and expectations
—discussion of mutually acceptable performance criteria and monitoring procedures
—establishing channels for communicating performance concerns to the vendor
—documenting all agreements
—maintaining a positive attitude including frequent reminders that librarians find few agencies to be perfect and that agency performance should be assessed against the standard performance of other agencies rather than against some idealized concept of the perfect vendor.

tionship, failure can occur because the "chemistry" is not right.[111]

There is no litmus test a library can apply to predict the fit with a specific vendor, and the elements that make up the mix change over time. While a positive reaction enhances a library's view of a vendor and the quality of the service it provides, such a spark does not appear to be a prerequisite for a successful library-agency relationship. On the other hand, a negative reaction should serve as a warning sign to the library to consider another vendor if others offer comparable coverage, service, and pricing or it should at least provide advance warning to overhaul safety measures if there is no acceptable alternate supplier. Appropriate safety measures include: vigilance in setting out the library's service requirements and expectations, discussion of mutually acceptable performance criteria and monitoring procedures, establishing channels for communicating performance concerns to the vendor, documentation of all agreements, and a positive attitude that includes frequent reminders that librarians find few agents perfect. Agency performance should be assessed against the standard performance of other agents rather than against some idealized concept of the "perfect" vendor.

SOME THINGS THAT ANNOY

—Timing of invoices
—Supplemental invoices
—Orders based on bids or quotes
—Statements
—Agency renewal lists and publishers' renewal notices
—Renewal pricing discrepancies
—Expiration dates and subscription terms
—Multiple copy orders
—Receipt of duplicates
—Cancellations and refunds
—Merges and splits
—Address changes
—Payment of agency invoices and problem resolution
—Agency lists and reports
—Back issue sets and single issue back orders

COMMON ANNOYANCES

In even the best library-agency relationship, there will be areas in which the fit between library, agency, and publishers is less than perfect. This section describes some of the more common sources of annoyance and strategies to reduce their impact on library operations.

Agency capabilities vary. The extent of variation often depends on the sophistication and flexibility of an agency's internal automated system. Librarians tend to assess agency systems in terms of their ability to accommodate variations of direct significance to libraries. In practice, library perceptions of the quality of agency service are equally dependent upon the extent to which agency systems can accommodate the varied requirements of different publishers.

While human intervention is almost always possible, the economic viability of an agency depends upon the application of automated procedures to all orders. A small agency with annual revenues of $15 million might process 300,000 to 350,000 orders a year, while a large agency with revenues of $300 million could process 2.5 to 3 million subscriptions. In practical terms, treating an order as an exception is only feasible when the appropriate exception routines have been programmed as options in the agency's automated system. The costs of manual intervention for exception handling of even half of one percent of orders would be prohibitive. It is theoretically possible to do almost anything with an automated system; however, it is not economically viable to support ad hoc custom programming and patching to support non-standard procedures for a limited number of orders or libraries.

TIMING OF INVOICES

In libraries where administrative procedures for paying invoices are complex and time-consuming, the receipt of a single agency invoice in place of separate invoices from multiple publishers can represent significant savings. The benefits of these savings can be blurred if agency invoicing schedules result in a library receiving its invoice at a time when its administration is stressed by an influx of annual invoices from other sources or during an intense budget preparation cycle. Delays occasioned by log-jams of paper work can cost money—in the form of late payment charges or the loss of service charge discounts that are tied to the timely settlement of invoices.

Most North American subscription agencies produce consolidated annual invoices for their calendar year customers between June and October. [Many European agencies issue consolidated invoices on a more frequent basis, billing renewals as invoices are received from publishers throughout the year.] If the timing of an annual invoice is of concern to a library, most agencies can make exceptions to their normal billing cycle and generate invoices on a schedule more suitable for the library. A library should inform its agency of any special scheduling requirements during initial discussions on service provision. If left until later, an agency may not be able to implement a timely adjustment.

The earlier in the year an agency generates an invoice, the greater the likelihood that the invoice will show subscription rates lower than those that actually apply for the upcoming subscription year. There is no pattern to the timing of publishers' announcements of subscription price increases, but many publishers operate on a subscription year that parallels the calendar year. The closer a new subscription year is, the greater the probability that agency files will have been updated to show the rates that apply for that year.

While welcomed by most libraries, consolidated annual invoices do not meet the needs of all libraries. Particularly in situations where common expiration dates have not or cannot be established, librarians may find administrators reluctant to authorize payment of invoices that contain items that are not due to expire for some months. In such situations, a library can request that renewal notices and invoices be issued on a more frequent schedule—monthly or quarterly, for instance—thus allowing it to retain the savings that accrue from paying an agent rather than multiple individual publishers while accommodating the concerns of corporate managers.

SUPPLEMENTAL INVOICES

Libraries that find the convenience of a consolidated invoice an attractive reason for using subscription agency services are frequently disturbed by the receipt of multiple supplemental invoices covering rate changes announced after the preparation of the annual invoice or new subscriptions. Most agencies are willing to work with libraries to diminish the impact of supplemental invoices. The most common approach is to combine multiple supplemental billings and issue them on a regular library-defined schedule—once a month, quarterly, etc. For an additional service charge, some agencies will absorb all price increases announced after the generation of a library's annual invoice (and, if such billings do not reach the expected level, some agencies will refund unexpended funds at the end of the period). Libraries with the ability to arrange rapid payment of annual invoices can reduce the number of supplemental billings attracted by their lists by arranging for their invoices to be issued late in the agency's billing cycle. The later in the year an invoice is generated, the greater the likelihood that the rates invoiced will be those that apply for the next subscription year.

ORDERS BASED ON BIDS OR QUOTES

Because publishers report subscription rate changes throughout the year, a library submitting an order based on a bid or quote obtained several months earlier should expect that the agency invoice for the order will exceed the amount originally quoted. Both the agency and library will benefit if purchase orders for such transactions can be written to authorize expenditures "not to exceed [the amount of the bid or quote] plus [a specified percentage]." The appropriate percentage will vary according to the type of material in the library's list and the amount of time between preparation of the bid or quote and submission of the order. If the time lag is six months or more, a ten percent variance should be appropriate; for a shorter time lag, five percent may suffice.

STATEMENTS

Agencies typically issue statements on a monthly basis when there is an outstanding debt or credit balance or whenever there has been activity on an account. As most libraries pay from invoices, the utility of account statements can be easily overlooked. If presented in a format that facilitates understanding, such statements can be useful management tools for tracking library expenditures and agency billings. Most libraries find statements that show invoice numbers and dates, library purchase order numbers and/authorizations, credit note numbers and dates, and the dates and check numbers for payments made by the library to be more helpful than bald statements of the current debit or credit balance. If the format of an agency's standard statement does not meet the local needs of a library, it should discuss alternate formats with the agency.

AGENCY RENEWAL LISTS AND PUBLISHERS' RENEWAL NOTICES

It is standard practice for North American subscription agencies to alert libraries to the need to renew agency-managed subscriptions by distributing consolidated renewal lists five to six months before the expiration of current subscriptions, and prior to generation of annual invoices. A library's renewal list contains all orders the agency has scheduled for renewal for the forthcoming year. Libraries check the listings by annotating them to identify titles to be cancelled rather than renewed and to suspend renewal on titles with severe publication delays. They return the marked-up listings to agencies as a signal for renewals to be placed with publishers. Agencies issue invoices reflecting these amended renewal lists. Given this procedure, many librarians are annoyed to receive renewal notices from publishers for titles handled by an agency.

Few libraries place all their subscriptions through agencies. For titles ordered direct from publishers, the only external signal of the impending expiration of a subscription is the publisher's renewal notice or invoice. Unless these renewals are identified and processed, the subscriptions will lapse. Most publishers are anxious to ensure that expiring subscriptions are renewed and are concerned to collect renewal revenues as early as possible. Publishers' renewal procedures typically comprise a set of mailings that begin months in advance of the expiration of a subscription. Although the cost of renewal mailings can be significant—over $1.00 per piece per subscriber—that does not deter some publishers from pursuing renewal cycles that include six or more mailings. The deluge of renewal notices can be a source of considerable work and annoyance for libraries.

Because renewal notices for titles ordered direct must be identified and processed, libraries cannot afford to ignore publishers' renewal alerts. Yet, for most libraries, the majority of the notices will be superfluous as they cover titles handled by an agency. The best solution to the problem of publisher renewal notices is to have knowledgeable staff who can readily distinguish between notices for items that the library acquires through agencies and those for items that are ordered direct. The latter can be retained for processing and most of the former can either be discarded or held to check against agency renewal lists to confirm prices and expiration dates. If publisher notices for titles handled by an agency are checked, follow-up should be initiated if a renewal notice shows an expiration date that differs from that reported by the agency by more than one month.

Agencies have had little success in persuading publishers to cease issuing renewal notices for subscriptions processed by agents. Most publishers do not distinguish library subscriptions from those for other subscribers. Even if they could, it is debatable whether they would be prepared to refrain from direct solicitation of renewals. Agencies have had some success in educating publishers for whom agency orders represent a high proportion of total sales. Given the costs of renewal solicitation and the fact that library orders have a high rate of renewal, some of these publishers delay renewal activities by several months until the bulk of agency orders are received and limit the number of mailings in their standard renewal sequences.

RENEWALS FOR SUBSCRIPTIONS FOR INDIVIDUALS

Publisher renewal procedures can cause severe headaches for corporate and special libraries that manage subscriptions for individuals. Publishers send their renewal notices to the shipping addresses to which issues are sent rather than to the billing addresses which are the usual focus of agency renewal activities. Individual subscribers receive the publishers' renewal notices. If the subscriber is aware of the appropriate procedure, the notice will be forwarded to the library for action. If the title is acquired through an agency, the library will check its most recent invoice or renewal list to ensure that the subscription information is accurate and that the renewal will be handled by the agency. Meanwhile, the subscriber receives a second renewal notice, and then a third! The user's perceptions of the efficiency of the library can be jeopardized. There is little that a library can do other than make sure that users are informed of standard renewal procedures.

More concrete problems can emerge if an individual subscriber is not aware that personal subscriptions are handled by the library. In this situation, the subscriber receives a renewal notice, decides that the subscription should be renewed, and passes the notice to the purchasing department for renewal. Meanwhile, the library also processes the subscription for renewal through its agency. Four months later, the individual subscriber is receiving two copies of the title. If the subscriber approaches the publisher to sort out this problem by cancelling or changing one or both subscriptions, the results can be a real problem for the library. If the library's order is handled by a subscription agency, the agency may be perceived as the cause of the problem even though it was not involved in the chain of events. Again, the only recourse for the library is user education and liaison with the institutional purchasing department.

RENEWAL PRICING DISCREPANCIES

On some occasions, library staff will notice discrepancies between the subscription price for a title shown on an agency invoice, the subscription price shown in current issues of the title, and the price shown on publisher renewal notices. Such discrepancies are usually caused by differences in the subscription year for which the rate applies. The rate shown on the agency invoice will typically be that for the next subscription year; the subscription price printed in current issues of a title will be for current year subscriptions; and the rate shown on publisher renewal notices may be that for renewals entered immediately.

Publisher renewal notices often offer subscribers discount rates for subscription renewals placed before the current subscription expires—1990 subscription rates for 1991 renewals received in October, November, or December of 1990, for instance. Such offers can represent significant savings over the renewal rates shown on an agency's invoice. Libraries with the ability to prepay agency invoices and collections rich in titles that attract discounts for early renewal understandably expect that agencies will place their renewals in time to obtain the most favorable rates. Most agencies can indeed process and pay orders within the required time frame. However, an agency can experience considerable difficulty if its automated system does not support logic to allow the differential application of subscription rates. Possible solutions include separate, earlier invoicing of these titles or pre-selection screening of agencies to ensure that their systems can support the required subscription options.

EXPIRATION DATES AND SUBSCRIPTION TERMS

It is standard practice for agencies to establish common expiration dates for the subscriptions they handle. Although agent's publicity materials frequently present common expiration dates as being of advantage to libraries, the authors are uncertain as to what benefits the practice offers. Establishing a common expiration date for all titles in an account has clear advantages for an agency: it simplifies the compilation of consolidated annual invoices and facilitates coordination of automated processing and renewal.

In this and all other matters relating to the term of a subscription, agencies work within the parameters established by publishers. Publisher policies can result in an agency establishing subscription terms that differ from those requested by a library. Librarians often express concern about the efficiency of an agent when renewal lists or invoices show a subscription term different from that requested by the library. Some agencies have programmed their systems to recognize these variances and include explanation on their invoices and renewal lists; other agencies do not have such capabilities.

If a library places an order for a new subscription in March, the order is entered into the agency's system which accesses the appropriate customer and publisher profiles to determine the library's preferred expiration date, the type of publication, and the publisher's policies for order placement and the subscription term on that title. The library's profile indicates that new orders are to be placed for a calendar year with expiration scheduled for December. The publisher/title files show that the title is a consumer magazine for which back orders are not accepted, that subscriptions of less than one year are not available (but that odd term subscriptions of more than one year but less than two years are processed), and that new subscriptions become operational approximately six weeks after the publisher's receipt of the order. Taking these factors into account, some agency systems will generate an order for a twenty month subscription beginning in May and will create payment and invoicing entries for 1-8/12 times the annual subscription price.

If the same library submitted another new order in May for a title for which short-term subscriptions were accepted, some systems would still generate an order for a subscription term longer than a year. This might occur if the system determined that the library's renewal list was to be generated during the period when the new order was being processed by the agency— scheduling that would result in the title being excluded from the list of subscriptions to be renewed for the next calendar year. In this case, some systems automatically generate an initial order for the remainder of the current calendar year *and* for the next calendar year to ensure continuity of supply. The scheduling conflict applies only for the first renewal list; the title would revert to a standard calendar year subscription at the expiration of the initial subscription and would be included on future renewal lists.

If a library indicates that all orders are to be placed for the full calendar year in which they are submitted and the publisher accepts back issue orders for the current subscription period, new orders will request full subscription period coverage irrespective of the month in which the order is placed. Accordingly, payment and invoicing will be based on the full subscription term, regardless of whether the library submits the order in April or November.

That the examples in this section refer to month as the issue designator rather than volume is indicative of the bias of many agency systems, which are often designed to support calendar designations rather numeric issue identifiers. This can be an inconvenience for libraries such as law libraries, which typically structure their procedures around numeric issue identification. A library with this preference should research the designation capabilities and accuracy of a potential supplier's internal automated system.

MULTIPLE COPY ORDERS

Despite the apparent simplicity of the concept, multiple copy orders cause problems for many publishers. Problems are most common when multiple copies are shipped to a single address. In addition, problems occur frequently when a library seeks a change in the number of copies of a title on order during the term of the order: an order for an extra copy of a title may be treated as an extension to the subscription for a copy the library is already receiving, or cancellation of a copy may result in suspension of all of the library's orders for that title. While agencies are aware of these difficulties, there is little they can do to guarantee correct processing by publishers. [Libraries can limit the potential for problems by ensuring that all orders for a specific title are placed with the same agency. Many observers also advise that all orders for titles from one publisher should be placed with one agency.]

A library can limit the difficulties it experiences with multiple copy orders by alerting the agent when a transaction (order, change, cancellation, or claim) involves a title for which the library has multiple orders and by requiring that the agency include this information in its communications with publishers. Agency alerts to publishers should be explicit: "NEW ORDER FOR A SECOND COPY TO THIS ADDRESS," "LIBRARY ORDERS SIX COPIES, CANCEL ONLY SECOND COPY TO THIS ADDRESS," "LIBRARY ORDERS THREE COPIES, CLAIM IS FOR BRANCH LOCATION," or "LIBRARY ORDERS 12 COPIES, ADDRESS CHANGE AFFECTS ALL THREE COPIES GOING TO CENTRAL LOCATION."

Should a change in a multiple copy order result in a distribution problem, claiming and resolution will be facilitated if the library includes the relevant address labels with its request for correction.

RECEIPT OF DUPLICATES

The receipt of more copies of a title than a library has ordered is a signal to check the status of the order. The need for urgency depends upon the nature of the order, the frequency of publication of the title, and the period for which duplicates are received. Duplicates may result from incorrect interpretation of a request for change in a multiple copy order, premature activation of a renewal order, a publisher's extension of the term of an existing subscription in response to claims for missing issues, or errors by agencies or publishers.

If the duplication involves a periodical serial for which a library has a multiple copy order that has recently been adjusted, the order should be checked thoroughly as soon as duplicates are detected. If there have been no recent changes in the order, the urgency of action depends upon the frequency of publication of the title and any information provided on the address label on the duplicate material. For titles published monthly or more frequently, an occasional duplicate is not necessarily cause for alarm. No action need be taken unless the duplication continues or the address label contains an expiration date significantly different from that shown in the library's records. If the duplicate appears at the beginning of a new subscription year or volume, it is usually caused by the publisher extending the subscription because of a claim or starting a renewal subscription before the expiration of the current subscription. Agency renewal procedures are such that the next renewal should be in place in time to cover a matching missing issue at the end of the current subscription. A library that orders direct will be able to make its own assessment of the probable effect of its renewal schedule on the issue at the tail of the prematurely activated renewal.

The situation is different for periodical serials published less frequently—four or six times a year, for example—and for very expensive titles. In these cases, receipt of a duplicate at the beginning of a subscription period is likely to result in a matching missing issue at the end of the period, a gap unlikely to be covered by the timing of the next scheduled renewal. Again, address labels can be of assistance in identifying and resolving the problem. If possible, include the address labels from the regular and duplicate receipts in any correspondence with the agency or publisher.

Duplication of receipts for non-periodical serials normally involves relatively expensive materials and requires resolution to avoid problems of duplicate billing. A library planning to change suppliers for non-periodical serials should address the appropriate handling of duplicate receipts with both the old and new supplier, and seek to establish return and credit arrangements for duplicates arising from the change of suppliers.

CANCELLATIONS AND REFUNDS

Just as publishers have different policies for subscription start dates, they vary in their approaches to mid-term subscription cancellations. [Libraries do not usually experience difficulties with cancellations implemented by nonrenewal of a subscription. However, if a subscription is on a "'til forbid" basis, cancellation action must be initiated by the library informing its vendor that it wishes to cancel the title.] Some publishers will not accept mid-term cancellations, and some will not refund money for the unused portion of a subscription.

Subscription agencies do not control publishers' cancellation and refund policies; they will process cancellations to publishers and refund any credits they receive. Cancellation processing follows a path similar to that for new order placement. A library requesting a mid-term cancellation should allow at least two weeks for agency processing, and an additional six weeks for the cancellation to be effected by the publisher. Some agencies levy charges for processing mid-term cancellations.

Many agencies issue credits for cancellations if they are notified of the cancellation after issuance of an invoice but before payment has been forwarded to the publisher. If a cancellation is required because of an agency error in ordering, a library can expect to receive an immediate credit for the full amount of the subscription regardless of whether the publisher has been paid. The availability and timing of refunds or credits for other cancellations depends upon publishers' policies. If a refund is provided, it usually takes some time for it to be forwarded to the agency and credited to the library.

Agencies vary in their approaches to service charges assigned to cancelled titles. If the cancellation is due to an agency error, the service charge will be waived. Many agencies will also waive the service charge if notified of a cancellation before payment is made to the publisher. Most retain the service fee if not advised of the cancellation until the order has been dispatched to the publisher. Both libraries and agencies find that non renewal of an expiring subscription is the most convenient approach to cancellation.

When a title ceases publication, most agencies will pass on to libraries any credits they obtain from the publisher. Libraries are rarely reimbursed for the service charges on ceased titles, and some vendors levy a handling fee on any refunds received.

MERGERS AND SPLITS

Just as agencies do not control publishers' policies on cancellations, they cannot influence their treatment of existing subscriptions when publications split or merge. Most publishers notify their subscribers of such changes directly and advise them of their options for assignment of the remainder of current subscription monies. Libraries are frequently better informed about the options than are agencies. To ensure smooth implementation of the supply option chosen, a library should notify its agency of the change and any action that has been taken.

ADDRESS CHANGES

Address changes cannot be implemented overnight, nor can a library or agency control the timing of a publisher's implementation of an address change. Accordingly, address changes should be in the hands of publishers at least six weeks in advance of the date on which the change is to be activated, and the library should ensure that receipt procedures are maintained at the old address for some time and established at the new address several weeks in advance of the requested date of change. Requests for address changes should clearly distinguish both the old and new addresses.

PAYMENT OF AGENCY INVOICES AND PROBLEM RESOLUTION

An agency's annual invoice crystallizes many of the problems and frustrations libraries experience with subscription agency services. In one document, the invoice shows the amount of money a library spends on serials, the agency's service charge or discount, and an item by item listing of titles, subscription terms, and prices. In reviewing this document, all but the most casual observer will be able to identify apparent discrepancies—subscription terms that differ from those requested, prices higher than those shown on the agency's pre-invoice renewal list, the omission of new orders, and others. Thus, an agency invoice can present the alarming prospect of thousands of dollars about to go out the door on a service that appears not only to be full of holes but also to be on the verge of creating havoc with the library's supply of serials. The temptation is to pick up the phone, rage at the agency, and withhold payment until a new invoice on which all discrepancies have been explained or adjusted arrives.

Although this may be an understandable reaction, it is not a reasonable reaction. A knowledgeable serials manager will recognize that the majority of apparent problems are only apparent and that the agency service charge is the one agreed upon in recent negotiations, the subscription terms shown are those that have worked for the library in previous years, the subscription price increases are at the anticipated level, and, while the absence of a new order should be checked, the agency routinely places new orders activated during the renewal cycle on odd term subscriptions to ensure continuing service. The manager will also be aware that the invoice is a notice of agency intentions and that adjustments can be made, and that agency operations and its service to the library are based on the expectation that the invoice will be paid in full in the agreed time frame.

Unless the invoice presents an interpretation of the library's service needs that is totally at odds with previous service and agreements, it should be processed for payment while inquiries are pursued about any potentially serious errors. Such inquiries will be most rapidly resolved if addressed to the agency's service department rather than to its accounting office. The accounting office processes and dispatches the invoice; service department personnel have direct access to client, publisher, and title files, and know how to interpret these resources. Should the investigation reveal that there is a major problem with the invoice, it may be appropriate to negotiate a partial payment of the account, withholding full payment until the difficulty has been corrected. Agency viability and the costs of agency services to libraries are adversely affected by prolonged delays in invoice settlement.

AGENCY LISTS AND REPORTS

Most agencies support a variety of formats for their standard reports and listings. If a library finds that the format of the reports it receives from its agency cause inconvenience in internal processing and record keeping, it should discuss other format options with its agency. Among the elements that an agency may be able to adjust readily are:

- the number of copies produced.
- the selection criteria for records included in reports: all orders, all items with a specific billing address, all items for specified ship-to addresses; all orders, or single copy order, or multiple copy orders; all U.S. imprints, or all non-U.S. imprints; all orders for periodical serials and all orders for non-periodical serials; etc.
- the order in which records are sorted. Common options include: agency form of title, agency title number, library-assigned account codes, etc.
- the record elements included. This feature is most often adjustable by exclusion: a library requests that data elements the agency includes in standard reports be deleted from reports for the library. It is more difficult for most agencies to add new data elements to standard reports.
- the frequency of report generation. Many agencies support several options for the frequency of issue of standard reports and listings.
- the output format of reports. Individual library procedures may be such that a report usually issued in the form of individual slips would be easier to use if generated as a list output in date order, or reports issued as listings might be easier to use if formatted as a series of single item slips.

BACK ISSUE SETS AND SINGLE ISSUE BACK ORDERS

United States agencies rarely accept back orders for single issues of serials, and most limit back issue set orders to the calendar year preceding the start date of a new order. The larger U.S. agencies provide some assistance to libraries seeking more extensive back sets by supporting varying degrees of access to dealers specializing in back sets. Such support ranges from electronic mail linkages with a vendor to online access to selected vendor's catalogs. At least one agency provides support for clients seeking single issues of high demand titles in the form of a missing issue bank. Some libraries find that European agencies are more responsive to back set orders than are their U.S. counterparts.

KEEPING UP TO DATE

Whether we like it or not, change is a constant in serials acquisitions. If the events at the beginning of the decade set the tone, the 1990s will be a period of significant change in the established patterns of relationships between publishers, libraries, and serial vendors. Many of the practices and procedures accepted as standard in 1990 will undergo radical change or extinction in the coming years; this book presents but a snapshot in time of a constantly moving landscape. The challenge for the serials manager is to access and assimilate new information and modify policies and procedures to accommodate that data.

Serials librarians enjoy two significant advantages in the struggle to keep up-to-date: ready access to serials, the form of publication most suited to the distribution of timely information; and membership in a group of committed professionals—librarians, publishers, and vendors—ready, willing, and able to communicate and share their insights and experience.

In reflection of general concern about the availability of serials materials in libraries, reports on topics relating to serials acquisitions currently receive wide coverage in the general library literature. Serials acquisitions are also featured regularly in journals covering professional specialties such as acquisitions and collections development, cataloging and technical services, public services, and library administration as well as in the literature focussing on different types of libraries such as college, academic, medical, public, school, and special libraries. Particularly useful in providing an overview of recent writing in serials acquisitions is the annual survey, "The Year's Work in Serials, . . ." published in

Library Resources & Technical Services.[112] However, the broadest and deepest coverage is found in serials devoted to serials. Among the titles currently of importance are *Advances in Serials Management,*[113] the *Serials Librarian,*[114] and *Serials Review.*[115] Two less formal publications offer particularly timely coverage: *Against the Grain*[116] and the *Newsletter on Serials Pricing Issues.*[117]

Worldwide, several hundred vendors offer libraries services for the acquisition of serials materials. In addition to the companies readily identifiable as serials subscription agencies, book jobbers and specialist firms offer acquisition support for non-periodical serials, government documents, and foreign serials. Others focus on the supply of serials in particular formats, including microform and CD-ROM. Details of specific suppliers can be found in a number of publications, including *International Subscription Agents: an Annotated Directory* published by the American Library Association and currently in its fifth edition (1986) and *Literary Marketplace: the Directory of American Book Publishing with Names and Numbers* and *International Literary Marketplace,* annuals published by R.R. Bowker. However, none of these publications provides any assessment of vendor quality or reliability. Other librarians are the best source for identifying viable potential vendors.

As with the literature of serials acquisitions, opportunities for collegial communication occur at all forums attended by librarians, vendors, and/or publishers—national, regional, and local library and publishing conventions and meetings of groups with a special interest in serials or acquisitions. Currently, two of the most informative special interest groups for serials managers are the North American Serials Interest Group (NASIG),[118] which sponsors an annual conference in June, and the Charleston Conference,[119] which assembles in Charleston, South Carolina, usually in November. The proceedings of recent NASIG conferences have been published in the *Serials Librarian.*

Conference attendance requires time and money, and conferences never seem to be scheduled when you need them. All serials managers have access to two even more valuable resources—an inquiring mind and a practiced dialling finger. The responsible manager makes use of both to tap the vast resources of information available from other librarians, vendors, and publishers.

REFERENCES

1. David C. Taylor, *Managing the Serials Explosion* (White Plains, NY: Knowledge Industry Publications, Inc., 1982), p. 5.

2. Kit Kennedy, "The Cost of Global Serials: The Vendor's Perspective," in *Pricing and Costs of Monographs and Serials: National and International Issues,* ed. Sol H. Lee (New York, NY: Haworth Press, 1987), p. 79.

3. Jan Derthick and Barbara B. Moran, "Serial Agent Selection in ARL Libraries," *Advances in Serials Management* 1 (1986): 14-15.

4. Neither of which is a new phenomenon. Luke Swindler indicates that the "increase in the number of journals has been fairly constant over the past three centuries, with the total doubling every fifteen years" in Marcia Tuttle, *Introduction to Serials Management* (Greenwich, CT: JAI Press, 1983), p. 18.
   Ann Okerson references a 1927 report which found "Many instances . . . in which science departments were obliged to use all of their allotment for library purposes to purchase their periodical literature which was regarded as necessary for the work of the department." Ann Okerson, "Periodical Prices: A History and Discussion," *Advances in Serial Management* 1 (1986): p. 101.

5. Robert L. Houbeck, Jr., "If Present Trends Continue: Responding to Journal Price Increases," *Journal of Academic Librarianship* 13, no. 4 (1987): 214.

6. Charles Hamaker, "Journal Pricing: A Modest Proposal," *Serials Librarian* 11, nos. 3/4 (1987): 173.

7. Anne Okerson, "Periodical Prices: A History and Discussion," op. cit., includes a detailed discussion of these prices indexes.

8. For an examination of the relationship between industry-wide indexes and a local library price index see Mary E. Clack and Sally F. Williams, "Using Locally and Nationally Produced Periodical Price Indexes in Budget Preparation," *Library Resources & Technical Services* 27 (1983): 345-356.

9. Gary J. Brown, *The Business of Scholarly Journal Publishing* (Westwood, MA: Faxon, January 1989), p. 1.

10. Charles Hamaker, "The Least Reading for the Smallest Number at the Highest Price," *American Libraries* 19, no. 9 (October 1988): 765.

11. Ibid.

12. John Tagler, "Counterpoint: a Publisher's Perspective," *American Libraries* 19, no. 9 (October 1988): 767.

13. Ibid.

14. Ann Okerson, "Report on the ARL Serials Project," *Serials Librarian* 17, nos. 3/4 (1990): 115.

15. Raymond E. Palmer, "Suggestions for a Partnership," *CBE Views* 12, no. 1 (1989): 8.

16. Margaret McKinley, "Vendor Selection: Strategic Choices," *Serials Review* 16, no. 2 (Summer 1990): 53.

17. Bill Katz and Peter Gellatly, *Guide to Magazine and Serial Agents* (New York: R.R. Bowker Company, 1975), p. 22.

18. This section draws heavily on Marcia Tuttle's "Magazine Fulfillment

Centers: What They Are, How They Operate, and What We Can Do About Them," *Library Acquisitions: Practice and Theory* 9 (1985): 41-49.

19. Rita Lerner, "The Professional Society in a Changing World," *Library Quarterly* 54, no. 1 (1984): 36-47.

20. Steven D. Zink, "Government Publications as Serials," in *The Serials Collection: Organization and Administration,* ed. Nancy Jean Melin (Ann Arbor, MI: Pierian Press, 1982), p. 115.

21. Rosemary Stevens, "Acquisition of Serials From Asia and Africa at the School of Oriental and African Studies (SOAS) Library," *Library Acquisitions: Practice & Theory* 7, no. 1 (1983): 63.

22. Ibid.

23. From time to time, listings of vendors specializing in government publications appear in the serials literature. See, for instance, Susan L. Dow, "A Selective Directory of Government Document Dealers, Jobbers and Subscription Agents," *Serials Librarian* 14, nos. 1/2 (1988): 157-186.

24. Margaret McKinley, "Vendor Selection: Strategic Choices," p. 52.

25. Tom Montag, "Stalking the Little Magazine," *Serials Librarian* 1, no. 2 (Spring 1977): 103.

26. Ibid.

27. Rosemary Stevens, "Acquisition of Serials From Asia and Africa," p. 65.

28. Ibid.

29. Vicky Reich, "Summary Session," *Serials Librarian* 17, nos. 3/4 (1990): 145.

30. For perspectives on the options from the research library viewpoint, see Sheila T. Dowd "Fee, Fie, Foe, Fum: Will the Serials Giant Eat Us?" *Journal of Library Administration* 10, no. 1 (1989): 17-38 and James C. Thompson, "Confronting the Serials Cost Problem," *Serials Review* 15, no. 1 (Spring 1989): 41-47.

31. See Huibert Paul, "Are Subscription Agents Worth Their Keep?" *Serials Librarian* 7, no. 1 (Fall 1982): 31-41.

32. Bill Katz and Peter Gellatly, *Guide to Magazine and Serial Agents,* p. 33.

33. Timothy W. Sineath, "Libraries and Library Subscription Agencies," *Library Scene* 1, no. 2 (Summer 1972): 28.

34. Betsy L. Humpreys, "Serials Control by Agents," in *Serials Automation for Acquisitions and Inventory Control,* eds. William Gray Potter and Arlene Farber Sirkin (Chicago: American Library Association, 1981), p. 64.

35. Betsy L. Humpreys, "Serials Control by Agents," p. 63.

36. This account is based on Edna Laughrey, "Acquisition Costs: How the Selection of a Purchasing Source Affects the Cost of Processing Materials," in *Pricing and Costs of Monographs and Serials: Naional and International Issues,* ed. Sul H. Lee (New York: Haworth Press, 1987), pp. 53-65.

37. See Stella Pilling, "The Use of Serials Subscription Agents by the British Library Document Supply Centre," *Serials Librarian* 14, nos. 3/4 (1988): 127-131.

38. See Stanley R. Greenfield, " . . . And the Subscription Agent," *Special Libraries* 63, no. 7 (July 1972): 293, 298-304.

39. "F. W. Faxon Co., Inc: The Computer is the Factory; The Product: Service," *Data Processor* (November 1976). Distributed as an advertising brochure by Faxon.

40. F. F. Clasquin, "Automation and the Subscription Agency," in *Management of Serials Automation,* ed. Peter Gellatly (New York: Haworth Press, 1982), p. 264.

41. Karen A. Schmidt, "Choosing a Serials Vendor," *Serials Librarian* 14, nos. 3/4 (1988): 14.

42. Betsy L. Humphreys, "Serials Control by Agents," p. 70.

43. Jane Baldwin and Arlene Moore Sievers, "Subscription Agents and Libraries: An Inside View of What Every Serials Librarian Should Know," *Advances in Serials Management* 2 (1988): 40.

44. J. B. Merriman, "The Work of a Periodicals Agent," *Serials Librarian* 14, nos. 3/4 (1988): 20.

45. R. J. Prichard, "Serial Acquisitions: the Relation Between Serials Librarian and Subscription Agent," *Serials Librarian* 14, nos. 3/4 (1988): 6.

46. Marcia Tuttle, "Can Subscription Agents Survive? *Canadian Library Journal* 42, no. 5 (October 1985): 261.

47. N. Bernard Basch, "Checking Out the Library Market: the Circulation Manager's Ally," *Circulation Management* 3, no. 5 (May 1988): 33.

48. Allen Press, Inc., *Journal Promotion Series* (mimeographed) (April 1983).

49. Frank F. Clasquin, "The Fiduciary Relationship of Libraries and Subscription Agencies," *Serials Librarian* 17, nos. 1/2 (1989): 41.

50. Bill Katz and Peter Gellatly, *Guide to Magazine and Serial Agents,* p. 65.

51. Richard W. Boss and Judy McQueen, "The Use of Automation and Related Technologies by Domestic Book and Serial Jobbers," *Library Technology Reports* 25, no. 2 (March-April 1989): 125-251.

52. Betsy L. Humphreys, "Serials Control by Agents," p. 75.

53. See Jane Maddox, Otto Harrassowitz in "Do Serial Vendor Policies Affect Serials Pricing?" ed. October Ivins, *Serials Review* 16, no. 2 (Summer 1990): 23-25.

54. Marcia Tuttle, *Introduction to Serials Management,* p. 78.

55. Ronald Akie, "Periodical prices: 1986-1988 update," *Serials Librarian* 15, nos. 1/2 (1988): 51.

56. The authors know of only one agency that provides information on remittance prices. Clients of the Faxon Company can access this data through the Datalinx service.

57. N. Bernard Basch and Alice Size Warner, "Subscription Agencies: a New Look at an Old Service," *Library Journal* 113, no. 6 (April 1988): 59.

58. Thomas R. Sanders, "Subscription Agents in an Automated World," *Serials Librarian* 14, nos. 3/4 (1988): 42-43.

59. Marcia Tuttle, "The Serials Manager's Obligation," *Library Resources & Technical Services* 31, no. 2 (April/June 1987): 138.

60. For the reactions of agencies, publishers, and librarians see "Do Serial Vendor Policies Affect Serials Pricing?" ed. October Ivins, pp. 7-27, 80.

61. John Breithaupt, Allen Press, Inc. in "Do Serial Vendor Policies Affect Serials Pricing?" ed. October Ivins, p. 10.

62. Stephen Horvath, Sage Periodicals Press in "Do Serial Vendor Policies Affect Serials Pricing?" ed. October Ivins, pp. 13-14.

63. Ibid.

64. Frank F. Clasquin, "The Subscription Agency and Lower Serials Budgets," *Serials Librarian* 1, no. 1 (Fall 1976): 39.

65. Timothy W. Sineath, "Libraries and Library Subscription Agencies," p. 30.

66. Marcia Tuttle, "Serials Control, from an Acquisitions Perspective," *Advances in Serials Management* 2 (1988): 71.

67. Bill Katz and Peter Gellatly, *Guide to Magazine and Serial Agents*, p. 94.

68. Ibid., p. 93.

69. Henry Kuntz, "Serials Agents: Selection and Evaluation," *Serials Librarian* 2, no. 2 (Winter 1977): 140.

70. Audrey Eaglen, *Buying Books* (New York: Neal-Schuman Publishers, Inc., 1989), p. 89.

71. Marcia Tuttle, *Introduction to Serials Management*, p. 78.

72. James T. Stephens, "The Library's Cost and the Vendor's Price for Serials," in *Pricing and Costs of Monographs and Serials: National and International Issues,* ed. Sul H. Lee (New York: Haworth Press, 1987), p. 94.

73. Phillip E. Greene, III, "The Three-Way Responsibility: Dealer-Publisher-Library," in *Management Problems in Serials Work*, eds. Peter Spyers Duran and Daniel Gore (Westport, CT: Greenwood Press, 1974), p. 96.

74. While the CEO of a major U.S. subscription agency recently indicated that it "differentiates its service charge for each title, based on . . . experience with that title," the comment was made in the context of "publishers who provide good financial terms" (discounts), rather than the amount of effort expended in servicing a title. See Richard R. Rowe, The Faxon Company in "Do Serial Vendor Policies Affect Serials Pricing?" ed. October Ivins, *Serials Review* 16, no. 2 (Summer 1990): 26.

75. Jan Baldwin and Arlene Moore Sievers, "Subscription Agents and Libraries," p. 43.

76. October Ivins, "We Need Department Store *and* Boutique Serials Vendors," *Serials Librarian* 17, nos. 3/4 (1990): 105.

77. Michael E. D. Koenig and Elizabeth A. Morse, "Sci-Tech Libraries and Serials Agents: the Unused Leverage," *Science and Technology Libraries* 5, no. 2 (Winter 1984): 35.

78. John Merriman, Dan Tonkery and Margaret M. Merryman, "Waiting for 'Nodough': the Future of Service Charges," *Serials Librarian* 17, nos. 3/4 (1990): 180.
For a discussion of unbundling from a library perspective, see Joseph W. Barker, "Unbundling Serials Vendors' Service Charges: Are We Ready?" *Serials Review* 16, no. 2 (Summer 1990): 33-43.

79. Thomas R. Sanders, "Subscription Agents in an Automated World," p. 41.

80. Doris E. New, "Serials Agency Conversion," *Serials Librarian* 2, no. 3 (Spring 1978): 279.

81. Marcia Tuttle, *Introduction to Serials Management*, p. 81.

82. Marcia Tuttle, "Serials Control, from an Acquisitions Perspective," p. 71.

83. Jan Derthick and Barbara B. Moran, "Serial Agent Selection in ARL Libraries," op. cit.
84. William H. Huff, "The Acquisition of Serial Publications," *Library Trends* 18 (January 1970): 294-317.
85. Marcia Tuttle, *Introduction to Serials Management,* pp. 81-82.
86. Jan Derthick and Barbara B. Moran, "Serial Agent Selection in ARL Libraries," p. 20.
87. Richard Jasper, "Performance bonds used to safeguard library deposits," *Against the Grain* 2, no. 1 (February 1990): 25-27.
88. Marcia Tuttle, "The Serial Manager's Obligation," p. 137.
89. See Frank F. Clasquin, "The Claim Enigma for Serials and Journals," in *Management Problems in Serials Work,* eds. Peter Spyers-Suran and Daniel Gore (Westport, CT: Greenwood Press, 1974), pp. 66-88. Literature on the claiming experience of individual libraries includes Barbara A. Carlson, "Guilt-Free Automated Claiming," *Serials Review* 15, no. 4 (Winter 1989): 33-42 and Irene J. Wernstedt, "The Effectiveness of Serials Claiming," *Serials Review* 8, no. 1 (Spring 1982): 43-47.
90. See Frank F. Clasquin, "The Claim Enigma for Serials and Journals," pp. 72-75.
91. John Merriman, Don Tonkery, and Margaret M. Merryman, "Waiting for 'Nodough'," pp. 180-181.
92. Judith L. Rieke, "Online Claiming: What Benefits?" *Serials Review* 3 (November 1988): 30 and Barbara A. Carlson, "Guilt-Free Automated Claiming," p. 40.
93. Frank F. Clasquin, "The Claim Enigma for Serials and Journals," p. 68.
94. Lawrence R. Keating, II, Nancy H. Rogers, and Bill Wilmering, "To Bid or Not to Bid: Is It Still a Choice?" *Serials Librarian* 17, nos. 3/4 (1990): 175.
95. See Jan Anderson, "Challenging the 'Good Buddies Factor' in Vendor Selection," *Advances in Serials Management,* 3 (1989): 153-171. Library managers considering the use of a formal bid process or investigating opportunities for reducing service charges by consolidating serials orders with a single vendor will find this account of the experience of Utah State University helpful. The article includes a copy of the USU request for proposal.
96. Lawrence R. Keating, II, Nancy H. Rogers, and Bill Wilmering, "To Bid or Not to Bid: Is It Still a Choice?" p. 175.
97. Jan Anderson, "Order Consolidation: A Shift to Single Vendor Serivce," *Serials Librarian* 17, nos. 3/4 (1990): 96.
98. Bill Katz and Peter Gellatly, *Guide to Magazine and Serial Agents,* p. 42.
99. Jan Derthick and Barbara B. Moran, "Serial Agent Selection in ARL Libraries," p. 29.
100. Jan Derthick and Barbara B. Moran, "Serial Agent Selection in ARL Libraries," p. 30.
101. Marcia Tuttle, "Serials Control, from an Acquisitions Perspective," p. 82.
102. Sharon C. Bonk, "Towards a Methodology of Evaluating Serials Vendors," *Library Acquisitions: Practice & Theory* 9 (1985): 52.
103. Ibid., p. 51.

104. Bill Katz and Peter Gellatly, *Guide to Magazine and Serial Agents,* p. 66.
105. Karen A. Schmidt, "Choosing a Serials Vendor," p. 12.
106. Robert L. Houbeck, Jr., in "Do Serial Vendor Policies Affect Serials Pricing?" ed. October Ivins, *Serials Review* 16, no. 2 (Summer 1990): 15.
107. Michael E. D. Koenig and Elizabeth A. Morse, "Sci-Tech Libraries and Serials Agents," p. 42.
108. Doris E. New, "Serials Agency Conversion in an Academic Library," *Serials Librarian* 2, no. 3 (Spring 1978): 282.
109. Bill Katz and Peter Gellatly, *Guide to Magazine and Serial Agents,* p. 34.
110. Ibid., p. 33.
111. Karen A. Schmidt, "Choosing a Serials Vendor," p. 15.
112. *Library Resources & Technical Serivces,* Chicago: Association for Library Collections and Technical Services, American Library Association.
113. *Advances in Serials Management,* Greenwich, CT: JAI Press, 1986-
114. *Serials Librarian,* ISSN: 0098-7913 Ann Arbor, MI: Pierian Press.
115. *Serials Librarian,* ISSN: 0361-526X Binghamton, NY: Haworth Press.
116. *Against the Grain,* ISSN: 1043-2094 Charleston, SC: Katina Strauch.
117. *Newsletter on Serials Pricing Issues,* Chicago: Publisher/Vendor-Library Relations Committee's Subcommittee on Serial Pricing Issues, Association for Library Collections and Technical Services, American Library Association.
118. NASIG (North American Serials Interest Group, Inc.) does not have an institutional address; contact is maintained through current officers. The President for 1990-91 is Mary Elizabeth Clack, Serial Records Librarian, Harvard College Library, Serials Records Division, Cambridge, MA 02138. Phone: (617) 495-2422; Fax: (617) 495-0403.
119. The Charleston Conference is organized by Katina Strauch, Head, Collection Development, College of Charleston Library, Charleston, SC 29424. Phone: (803) 792-8020/8008; Fax: (803) 792-8019/5505.

RECOMMENDED READING

Anderson, Jan. "Challenging the 'Good Buddies Factor' in Vendor Selection." *Advances in Serials Management* 3 (1989): 153-171.
Library managers considering the use of a formal bid process for subscription agency selection or investigating the opportunities for reducing service charges by consolidating serials orders with a single vendor will find this account of the experience of Utah State University helpful. The article includes a copy of USU's request for proposal.

———. "Order Consolidation: A Shift to Single Vendor Service." *Serials Librarian* 17, nos. 3/4 (1990): 93-97.
An update report on the results of Utah State's consolidation of subscriptions with a single vendor. Positive results include savings in service charges and staff time, and the clout attendant upon the size of the consolidated account.

Baldwin, Jane, and Arlene Moore Sievers, "Subscription Agents and Libraries: an Inside View of What Every Serials Librarian Should Know." *Advances in Serials Management* 2 (1988): 37-45.
Common sense nuts-and-bolts advice for establishing and maintaining smooth working relationships with serial vendors.

Barker, Joseph W. "Unbundling Serials Vendors' Service Charges: Are We Ready?" *Serials Review* 16, no. 2 (Summer 1990): 33-43.
A librarian's response to suggestions that serial vendors may be moving towards applying service charges on the basis of service use.

Basch, N. Bernard, and Alice Sizer Warner, "Subscription Agencies: a New Look at an Old Service." *Library Journal* 113, no. 6 (April 1988): 57-59.
A brief outline of the history of subscription agencies, service trends, and current vendors.

Bonk, Sharon C. "Towards a Methodology of Evaluating Serials Vendors." *Library Acquisitions: Practice & Theory* 9 (1985): 51-60.
One of the few articles that focuses on evaluation of vendor support for the acquisition of non-periodical serials. Includes discussion and check-lists of factors to be considered in vendor evaluation. Details the results of an evaluation of the price and delivery time performance of different (un-named) vendors supplying fifty-one non-periodical serials to twelve different medium and large academic libraries.

Clasquin, Frank F. "The Claim Enigma for Serials and Journals." In, *Management Problems in Serials Work*, edited by Peter Spyers-Duran and Daniel Gore, Westport, CT: Greenwood Press, 1974. pp. 66-88.
Detailed examination of library, agency, and publisher responsibilities for claims. While some of the procedural specifics are out-of-date, the piece provides a useful overview of claims management.

Derthick, Jan and Barbara B. Moran, "Serial Agent Selection in ARL Libraries." *Advances in Serials Management* 1 (1986): 1-42.
Surveys the use of serials vendors by major academic research libraries. Reports the factors of significance in the selection of vendors and identifies the vendors most frequently used for the acquisition of domestic and foreign serials.

Greenfield, Stanley R. ". . . And the Subscription Agent." *Special Libraries* 63, no. 7 (1972): 293, 298-304.
Straightforward discussion of the boundaries of subscription agency responsibility in the provision of basic subscription services. Old, but valid.

Humphreys, Betsy L. "Serials Control by Agents." In, *Serials Automation for Acquisitions and Inventory Control*, edited by William Gray Potter and Arlene Farber Sirkin, Chicago: American Library Association, 1981, pp. 57-76.
Describes the range of auxiliary services available from subscription agencies in the early 1980s and the use of agencies for subscription handling. While no longer comprehensive in detail, the piece is a readable discussion of options and alternatives, informed by the experience of the National Library of Medicine.

Ivins, October, ed. "Do Serial Vendor Policies Affect Serials Pricing?" *Serials Review* 16, no. 2 (Summer 1990): 7-27, 80.
Contributions from librarians, publishers, and vendors addressing the effects of vendor policies on serials prices. Provides rare coverage of subscription agency operations and pricing and publisher discounts to vendors.

Katz, Bill and Peter Gellatly. *Guide to Magazine and Serial Agents*, New York: R.R. Bowker Company, 1975.
Readable, informative, in-depth consideration of all aspects of the use of subscription agencies for the acquisition of periodical serials. Although the serials supply environment has changed significantly since the mid-1970s, Katz and Gellatly's common-sense approach still has relevance for librarians seeking to define their service needs and options.

New, Doris E. "Serials Agency Conversion," *Serials Librarian* 2, no. 3 (Spring 1978): 277-285.
Focuses on the consolidation of subscriptions with a single vendor. Discusses the rationale for consolidation, selection of the vendor, and vendor change procedures. Includes check-lists for vendor comparison.

Okerson, Ann. "Periodical Prices: a History and Discussion," *Advances in Serials Management* 1 (1986): 101-134.
Detailed review of the literature of periodical price surveys and price increases since 1970.

Paul, Huibert. "Are Subscription Agents Worth Their Keep?" *Serials Librarian* 7, no. 1 (Fall 1982): 31-41.
The consensus breaker that challenges the almost universal belief that use of subscription agency services saves libraries time and money. Advocates direct placing of orders with publishers. Not necessarily valid on specifics, but food for thought particularly for libraries with automated serials systems and the ability to generate checks quickly and inexpensively.

Pilling, Stella. "The Use of Serial Subscription Agents by the British Library Document Supply Centre," *Serials Librarian* 14, nos 3/4 (1988): 127-131.
Details the labor savings that BLDSC realizes through the use of subscription agencies for serials acquisition.

Rieke, Judith L. "Online Claiming: What Benefits?" *Serials Review* 3 (November 1988): 29-31.
Comparison of data entry times and claim response intervals of an unnamed vendor's online claim system against manual claiming procedures. The study was undertaken during initial testing of the online claim system and thus may not represent responsiveness under routine operational conditions.

Stephens, James T. "The Library's Cost and the Vendor's Price for Serials." In *Pricing and Costs of Monographs and Serials: National and International Issues* edited by Sul H. Lee, New York: Haworth Press, 1987, pp. 89-96.
Interesting insight into the philosophy of the President of EBSCO, one of the two largest serial subscription agencies. Strong call for librarians to approach their relationships with suppliers from the perspective of "one business person to another business person."

Tuttle, Marcia. "Magazine Fulfillment Centers: What They Are, How They Operate, and What We Can Do About Them," *Library Acquisitions: Practice and Theory* 9 (1985): 41-49.
Comprehensive description of the operations of fulfillment agencies which perform subscription management for the publishers of popular and consumer magazines. Highlights procedures that cause problems for libraries and offers suggestions for avoiding these difficulties.

APPENDIX

OVERVIEW OF THE AUTOMATED PRODUCTS AND SERVICES AGENCIES PROVIDE FOR SERIALS MANAGEMENT IN LIBRARIES

The automation of internal services is a given in all but the smallest subscription agencies. Most serial vendors have gone beyond internal automation to develop automated products and services to support serials acquisition and subscription management in libraries. Vendors' service offerings vary widely in extent, sophistication, and cost. Different vendors offer different products, and vendors' implementations of a service can differ radically. Such differences can have a significant effect on the utility of a service in a specific library situation.

Most serial subscription agencies provide automated products and services for libraries. It is beyond the scope of this publication to provide a comprehensive review of the offerings of *all* serial vendors. However, detailed information on the range of such products and services can be of assistance to libraries in defining or reviewing their serial supply options. No single vendor offers a package of automated products and services that is representative of the full range of options supported by the industry as a whole. However, when taken in combination, the products offered by the two largest subscription agencies—EBSCO Subscription Services and the Faxon Company—illustrate most of the capabilities for which agencies currently provide automated support.

HOW TO USE THIS APPENDIX

This Appendix illustrates the range of automated services and products that subscription agencies offer libraries. It provides:

- an overview of the types of automated products and services available from most serials vendors,
- detailed descriptions of the capabilities for which serial vendors frequently offer automated support to libraries, and
- information on how two different vendors have implemented automated support services for libraries.

The descriptions reflect services and pricing as of mid-1990. While there is little evidence to suggest that the range of automated serials management services offered by subscription agencies will change radically in the next few years, there will be changes in the capabilities and pricing of the products supported by specific vendors. If the services of the vendors described in this Appendix are of interest to a library, details of functionality and pricing should be checked with vendor representatives.

Libraries investigating automated support for serials acquisition and management can use the Appendix to identify the functions subscription agencies typically support. When a function of interest is identified, examination of the approaches used by the vendors described will provide a basis on which a library can develop a checklist of the capabilities appropriate to its particular situation. The checklist can be expanded through investigation of the services offered by other agencies. Libraries seeking automated support for serials should also investigate the products and services available from other, nonagency, sources. These include: the automated serial systems developed by library automation companies; the online files of serials data and the electronic messaging systems supported by bibliographic utilities and database service vendors; and the online ordering, union listing, and interlibrary lending systems available from bibliographic utilities.

The Appendix can also assist libraries that have no immediate interest in automation. The rigorous analysis required for successful automation can provide valuable insight in nonautomated situations. For example, review of the claim capabilities of an automated system can assist a library in defining the kinds of missing issues that cause problems in its manual operations.

EBSCO SUBSCRIPTION SERVICES

EBSCO's automated products and services for serials acquisitions and management include:

- printed management reports from the agency's internal automated system,
- the EBSCONET system, which supports online access to agency files and the online submission of orders and claims,
- the *Serials Directory* on CD-ROM, and
- automated system interfaces to support data access and exchange between the agency and libraries with local automated systems.

The company has established interfaces with publishers for the transfer of orders, claims and pricing and scheduling information. It also offers additional CD-ROM products less directly oriented to serials acquisition and control. Current offerings include *Magazine Article Summaries*, a periodical abstracting service, and two products based on Medline abstracts.

Management Reports: The automated system used for internal agency operations also supports the production of printed management reports for clients. Among the standard reports are title lists output in a variety of arrangements including: title, subscriber, department, library-specific control data, and custom sorts; lists of journals by abstracting and indexing service coverage; lists by country of publication; and Summary of Publications Ordered reports in various formats. The standard Summary of Publications Ordered report is output in title order. Other formats include output ordered by price, subscriber, and user-defined codes. A Historic Price Analysis Report is also available. It provides five-year comparative pricing information for the titles a library orders through EBSCO. The report shows subscription costs and annual percentage changes in price by title and the total percentage change in prices for the most recent five years.

The system accommodates a range of data elements likely to be of importance to individual accounts. The Summary of Publications Ordered by User-Defined Codes report uses this data to list all publications ordered by a library sequenced by user-defined codes. The codes can be applied to designate fund accounts, departments, disciplines, branch locations, or virtually any other variable that a library chooses to incorporate into its subscription records.

Some management reports are provided as part of the general serials acquisition service, and others are available as added price options.

EBSCONET: An interactive online system that may be accessed through leased lines or by dial access through Tymnet, EBSCONET supports:

- speed searching of agency title, publisher, and price files,
- online entry of claims and queries to publishers,
- online order entry,
- access to, and ordering from, the Missing Copy Bank,
- access to information on individual library orders—the Summary of Publications Ordered feature,
- TELMAIL electronic mail,
- electronic messaging to Kraus Reprint & Periodicals, Inc., and
- keyword and Boolean searching of bibliographic and subscription data through the EBSCO SEARCH function.

The system carries an annual access fee of $250 payable in advance, and a monthly fee of $25 per hour for non-WATS access or $40 per hour for WATS access. These prices include all telecommunications charges. The Summary of Publications Ordered service incurs an additional charge of $25 per month per 1,000 records.

The *speed searching* facility provides five rapid access approaches to information in the title, publisher, and price files. Each is activated by entering a four character mnemonic command followed by the search term. The searches and associated commands are:

- Title look-up (TITL)
- Title look-up with publisher name and address (TITP)
- Publisher name look-up (PUBL)
- Titles by publisher name (PUBT)
- Publication price list (PRIC)

For title look-up (TITL and TITP), the title is the search term, and for publisher name look-up, the search term is the publisher's name. Titles by publisher name and publication prices (PUBT and PRIC) are accessed by EBSCO-assigned publisher or title numbers, which can be determined through PUBL or TITL look-up.

Each search type returns a different display screen. Displays that include title data show the title together with subscription edition information such as: airmail, surface mail, microfiche, etc.; title number; and, where appropriate, publication status information such as "suspended" or "completed series with vol 2." Publisher information displays include publisher names and addresses. The publisher number is added to PUBL and PUBT output.

The publication price list (PRIC) display contains bibliographic and subscription data in addition to title and title number. If the title number entered as a search term represents an inactive title that has been cross-referenced to an active title, the system displays the pricing data for the title to which the reference is made and includes an indication of the cross-reference relationship in the display.

The *claim* function allows a library to record and transmit claims and queries relating to its subscriptions. Claim is activated by entering the claim command (CLAI) and the title number for the item being claimed. [The title number can be determined: by a speed search on TITL, TITP, or PUBT; by reference to the adhesive labels that EBSCO supplies for use on check-in records; or by reference to printed invoices and reports.] Claims are recorded using a two-character numeric code for the type of claim or query being submitted. The system supports 18 codes to cover common claim or query types including:

- issues not received
- no service received on this order
- duplicates being received
- damaged issues—replace
- expiration notices being received
- binder not supplied with issue
- receiving insufficient number of copies
- receiving too many copies
- wrong start date
- subscription began too soon/expiration date should be:
- verify expiration
- no extensions or back issues accepted—refund
- extension not accepted—supply back issues or refund
- supply missing issues—no issues received since _____
- request replacement copy for binding
- advise current publication schedule
- subscription cancelled—cease mailing
- extend for issues unavailable
- advise new expiration.

Additional codes accommodate a general note and requests for sample issues.

Claims submitted online are processed in one of two ways, depending on the capabilities of the publisher to whom the claim is addressed:

- publishers linked to the TELMAIL electronic mail system receive the claim in the form of an electronic mail message
- claims and queries for other publishers are printed at EBSCO and mailed to the publisher

For titles from publishers that provide journal dispatch information, the claim screen displays publication schedule data that may obviate the need for a claim/query. This data includes the volume and number of the most recently published issue and the date on which that issue was dispatched.

The *online ordering* function is accessed by keying the order command (ORDE) and the title number or title of the publication to be ordered. The system then prompts for entry of:

- term of subscription (1 YR, 2 YR, etc.),
- quantity required,
- subscription start date—in the form of a date, or up to eight characters of alphabetic data such as ASAP, FROMEX, etc.,

- type of order: N (new) or R (renewal),
- purchase order number, or NONE,
- subscriber code or subscriber address (up to fifty-seven characters), and
- special instructions for order processing. Three lines, each seventy-five characters in length, are provided for these instructions.

At the completion of order entry, the operator has the option of accepting, changing, or cancelling the order.

The *Missing Copy Bank* function (MCBL) provides search and ordering access to the inventory of items in the Missing Copy Bank, a store of back issues of some 2,000 titles including those covered by *Magazine Index*, *Readers' Guide to Periodical Literature*, *Education Index*, *Business Periodicals Index*, *Abridged Index Medicus*, EBSCO's *Magazine Article Summaries*, and selected titles from the *Brandon and Hill List*. The Missing Copy Bank allows libraries to obtain missing issues that are no longer available from the publisher. The Bank contains customer donations of duplicate or unneeded copies. There is no charge for items from the Missing Copy Bank.

The file is accessed by title number. If an appropriate listing is found, the item can be ordered by keying an "O" (for order), the number of the line describing the issue, the number of copies of the issue required, and the library's subscriber code.

The *Summary of Publications Ordered* option allows libraries to access information on their subscriptions from the order file which is updated on a weekly basis. The service carries a monthly charge of $25 per 1,000 records. Each record represents a single subscription and contains:

- subscriber account number,
- title name and title number,
- name and department/location of individual subscriber if applicable,
- quantity ordered,
- invoice number,
- subscription start date,
- HEGIS code, a six-character code used to identify each title by fund, cost center, subject, or any other variable defined by the customer,
- term of the subscription,
- subscription price,
- date order placed, and
- order number.

Records also include unique subscriber and department codes created to meet the needs of each account.

Once accessed by entry of the SUMM command, records in the Summary of Publications Ordered file can be searched by title number, HEGIS code, subscriber name or code, and unique search codes. Entry of the search code A (for "all") retrieves the full list of orders for the account number used in sign-on, displayed in title number order.

The name search option allows the truncation of subscriber names and displays an intermediate search screen to prompt for selection of the correct name if multiple names are retrieved. Title searches can be combined with other elements, including individual subscriber and HEGIS codes.

The TELMAIL electronic mail system allows users to communicate with EBSCO and with other users. The system also provides access to claim responses from certain publishers and transmits orders and quote requests to and from Kraus Reprint & Periodicals. The function is menu-driven, supporting the following options:

- send mail,
- read incoming mail,
- review TELMAIL sent,
- TELMAIL directory,
- help, and
- Kraus Reprint & Periodicals.

An experienced user can bypass the menu and access the required functions by direct commands.

The system accommodates messages of up to 30 lines of text, each containing up to 74 characters and offers three levels of message security or priority: high, low, and "eyes only." The user can specify the number of days a message is to remain in the system, from one to 99. The read function displays a list of all incoming mail and allows the user to view a specific message, all messages, high priority messages only, or all unread messages. Claim responses from publishers are identified by the use of "claim #" in the subject area of the incoming mail list.

TELMAIL includes an option to support communication with Kraus Reprint & Periodicals, a back issue dealer with a collection of over 20,000 serials titles including a large number of non-English language publications. Selection of the Kraus function retrieves a formatted screen that includes: lines for the user's name and address keyed by the user or inserted automatically by entry of the user's subscriber code; an order/quotation message identifier flag; and a message area of up to twenty-five lines.

EBSCO SEARCH supports keyword searching of the bibliographic and pricing data in title, publisher, and price files. The files contain some 210,000 title listings. The listings reflect the working environment of a subscription agency rather than the bibliographic approach of library files. The files include inactive records, records for material suspended or delayed, cross-reference records, and multiple records for single titles, reflecting the agency's concern to provide accurate pricing data for a variety of situations—different currencies, language editions, air and surface delivery, etc. The search capabilities for accessing the files include Boolean, range, and truncation features, together with the ability to specify the field to be searched. Users also have browse access to the terms indexed in each field.

The basic search command is FIND. When used without a field prefix to identify an alternate search domain, FIND locates specified term(s) in the title field of records. When a search is to be executed on fields other than title, the required fields are specified using two- or three-character alphabetic field prefixes. In addition to title, the following fields can be accessed by:

- abstracts and indexes* in which the title is listed
- subject category*
- country of origin*
- additional comments
- cost (the cost most frequently used by the majority of customers—usually the one year cost of a library subscription). For foreign, multi-year, and other rate information, titles need to be checked using the price function in the quick search option.
- CONSER control number
- format of publication
- frequency
- index*
- ISSN
- language*
- LC classification
- Dewey Decimal classification
- NLM classification
- Universal Decimal Classification
- inclusion in Missing Copy Bank
- publisher name
- publisher number
- record type, main or subsidiary. "Main" indicates that the

database contains only one record for a title or, if there are multiple records, it designates the record that contains data for surface delivery for U.S. subscribers. All other records are subsidiary records
- index published separately indicator
- status*—active, bill later, suspended, cross-reference, now called, etc.; combination of publication history, status, and subscription information
- term—length of the subscription, and
- title number

*Data in these fields is recorded in the form of codes or abbreviations.

Search terms may be truncated using a hyphen, and multiple terms can be combined using Boolean "AND," "OR," and "NOT" operators. Stop words are clearly indicated, and the system reserves certain terms for internal operation. Such reserved terms must be encased in single quotes to function as search terms.

The system saves the last ten searches executed in a session. These may be combined using Boolean logic and the search number to execute more complex searches. Previous searches can be modified by the addition of terms and operators without rekeying the original search.

EBSCO SEARCH supports range searching of numeric fields with the THRU command. Such searches may only be performed on the contents of one field at a time. The results of multiple range searches on different fields can, however, be combined in a search that references the previous searches. The system also supports comparison searching of numeric fields using "EQUAL," "LESS THAN," "LESS THAN OR EQUAL," "MORE THAN," "MORE THAN OR EQUAL," and "NOT EQUAL" operators. Comparison searching is resource-intensive and time-consuming, and EBSCO recommends that users try to meet their needs with range searching wherever possible.

At the conclusion of a search, the system displays the number of hits on each term and the number of records retrieved by the search. Hits are displayed using function keys or specific display commands.

The INDEX command provides access to lists of terms indexed in specific fields. As with FIND, the default index is title. The indexes of other fields may be accessed using a specific field prefix. Index displays include a count of the number of times each term appears in the index.

As noted in the description of the cost field, the files accessed by

EBSCO SEARCH do not contain exhaustive price and subscription data. The company recommends that EBSCO SEARCH be used to select the titles of interest and that full subscription data for these titles then be inspected using the price option in the speed search facility.

The Serials Directory: The CD-ROM *Serials Directory*, updated quarterly, contains records for some 114,000 serials titles. The records comprise bibliographic information, augmented by subscription data such as publisher name, address, phone and fax numbers, price, and journal circulation data. In addition, the file contains the CONSER MARC record for each title.

The Directory supports keyword searching with Boolean operators. It also provides browse access to the alphabetic indexes ("authority files") of journal titles, subject headings with "see" and "see also" references, publishers, and the abstracting and indexing services that cover the journals. The system supports the generation of bibliographies and orders. Data retrieved in browse mode can be retained and refined in query mode. Search strategies, results, and orders can be displayed online, printed, or stored to disk for later manipulation.

The system provides support for the output of machine-readable CONSER records on diskette. Records cannot be edited prior to output but data can be transferred in ASCII for manipulation by standard word processing and other software.

Index searches are initiated by accessing the relevant index and keying the lead characters of the term to be searched. More extensive queries are entered using the query profile screen template. The system is menu-driven, with options for each function displayed on a sidebar at the left of the screen. Searches can be constructed using words or phrases in any field, in subject fields, and in title fields. The system supports right truncation, wildcard characters in any position in a word, word adjacency, and proximity ("within 50 characters"). If neither proximity nor adjacency is specified, multiple terms entered on the same line are linked by Boolean "OR" logic, and terms entered on different lines are linked by "AND" logic. "NOT" logic can be defined in the any field and subject areas. Searches can be qualified by publisher, frequency, language, and country of publication, and may be limited to the titles to which a library subscribes. Previous queries can be incorporated into current searches using "AND," "OR," and "NOT" logic. The file may also be accessed by ISSN and CONSER record number.

Results are displayed as a numbered alphabetical list of titles together with country of publication and ISSN. The user can browse through the list, limit the display to local titles, view detailed citations, view CONSER records, mark titles for inclusion or exclusion from the display, and generate bibliographies or orders.

The detailed record display uses a labeled screen format to present bibliographic, subject, and publisher information including price, publisher name, address, fax and phone numbers, journal editor, journal circulation, advertising and book review indicators, availability in other formats, and a descriptive listing of contents provided by the publisher.

The system provides three labeled citation formats for the production of bibliographies: brief, detailed, and complete. The brief format includes subject, key title, title, series statement, ISSN, country, language, frequency, price, and publisher. The labels and order of entries—alphabetic by title—are retained when a bibliography is generated directly from the Directory.

A formatted screen is provided for order generation. The user keys the variable information—start date and purchase order number—and the system automatically inserts the ship-to-address, date, journal title, ISSN, CONSER number, and supplier (EBSCO). Orders may be either saved for review or electronic transmission via EBSCONET or printed at the terminal.

The *Serials Directory* is a directory; the parallel file of CONSER records is provided to assist libraries in applications such as cataloging and to supply additional library-oriented information such as key title, CODEN, etc. The alphabetic indexes and word searching capabilities access information in directory records, not the CONSER file. While there is some commonality between directory records and the CONSER records, some of the differences might hinder a user expecting to search a MARC-based file. Title searches in the *Serials Directory* access a range of different types of title data including title, brief title, variant titles and previous titles, an approach the *Directory* has in common with MARC-based files. Subject searches likewise access subject data, but it is the directory data assigned by EBSCO and reflects the vendor's subject categories rather than the Library of Congress Subject Headings.

The CONSER file can be accessed by ISSN or CONSER number, and the CONSER records for items retrieved by directory searches can be viewed by selecting the "Display CONSER Record" option (which can also be selected as the default display option for the system). The CONSER file cannot be accessed directly by keyword. The CONSER display format includes all variable field tags, indicators, and subfield codes. Fixed field data is presented in a labeled format. CONSER records may be printed in a brief format containing CONSER number, ISSN, and title, printed in full format as they appear on the screen, or saved to an ASCII file.

The system can be tailored to: implement password control to different functions, thus limiting access to capabilities such as the display of MARC-formatted records and the generation of orders; activate the local title option that causes titles to which the library subscribes to be highlighted in displays; and record the library name and address data used in orders and other outputs. The system also allows a library to specify certain system controls such as the ability to direct output to disk and to limit the number of titles printed in a bibliography. The local titles option can be activated by keying each title (up to fifty-five characters) and the ISSN, or the data can be input from a floppy disk of the library's orders supplied by EBSCO. The Directory includes an online tutorial, online help, a statistical use log, and a manual. A single copy subscription costs $495; discounts apply to multiple copies.

The Directory can be accessed from an IBM PC/XT or /AT or a compatible personal computer with 640 KB of RAM, a double-sided floppy disk drive, a hard disk of at least 10 MB, a CD-ROM player, a monitor and keyboard, and MS-DOS version 3.2 or higher. Users who choose to transmit orders to EBSCO online require a modem and communications software; a printer is necessary for the output of printed bibliographies and orders.

Library System Interfaces: EBSCO provides a number of services to support access to EBSCONET through other networks and to distribute data in formats that can be loaded into local automated systems: specialized serials systems, multifunction automated library systems, and PC-based office systems. The company's development of client interfaces focuses on five capabilities:

- retrospective conversion,
- invoice downloading,
- online ordering,
- online claiming, and
- the provision of gateways from local library systems to EBSCONET.

For clients with more than 200 subscriptions, there is a free *retrospective conversion* service, EBSCO/RETRO. Titles for which the library has current subscriptions with EBSCO are matched against records from the CONSER and MARC Serials tapes. Hits are distributed on tape together with a printed report of non-matched records. If a library can provide CONSER numbers for non-matched records, these will be re-searched and output to a separate tape. EBSCO reports that the hit rate for MARC records for the subscriptions placed by a typical university library averages 96 percent. Local data—title number, account data, and EBSCO to identify the source of the records—are added (in field 902, subfields a, b, and c) to the records during the extraction. Records are output in ASCII in the MARC format on 1600 or 6250 bpi magnetic tape, magnetic tape cartridge, or floppy disk. The records can be loaded into automated systems that support the loading of serials data in the MARC format.

EBSCO can provide *machine-readable invoices* to save libraries the effort of keying from printed invoices. There is no charge for the service, which is available in five physical formats:

- 3-1/2-inch floppy diskettes,
- 5-1/4-inch floppy diskettes,
- magnetic tape cartridge,
- 1600 BPI magnetic tape, and
- 6250 BPI magnetic tape.

Invoice data is output in two files: Customer Name and Address and Invoice Line Item. The records in each file have a fixed length of 640 bytes and contain fixed-length fields. Customer Name and Address records contain office, account, subscriber, name and address in lines 1 through 6, special name, special department, and the date the file was created. Invoice Line Item records contain fields for invoice date, customer PO number, title, ISSN, CONSER number, LC classification, Dewey classification, NLM classification, frequency, country of origin, HEGIS code, quantity, start date, term, price, comments, handling charge, and language.

Machine-readable invoices have been successfully loaded into a variety of automated systems including: Lotus 1-2-3 spreadsheet programs, database management systems such as dBase, and multi-function automated library systems including Data Trek's Card Datalog, Geac, Innovative Interface's INNOVACQ, the Sydney Library System, and NOTIS. In some cases, the invoice format can also be used to load serials data into systems that do not accept records in the MARC format.

EBSCO offers two approaches for accepting *machine-readable orders and claims* from local automated library systems. Users of systems with dial-up or gateway access to public data networks can access EBSCONET from their local system terminals and use its ordering and claiming functions to input and transmit the appropriate orders and claims. Such gateway linkage has been implemented on ALANET, and the capability has been installed by the Florida Information Resources Network (FIRN) as well as by a number of other systems.

Libraries that wish to use the order and claim formatting functions of their local systems can transmit the output data directly by dial access and data transfer, bypassing the EBSCONET system. EBSCO translates the data into its internal format. The capability is operational for a number of systems, including Data Trek's Card Datalog, the Sydney Library System, NOTIS, and WLN.

EBSCO works closely with automated library system vendors to facilitate the loading of data and the transmission of machine-readable orders and claims. The availability of interfaces changes daily as development, testing, and implementation are completed. Up-to-date information on the status of specific interfaces is available from EBSCO regional offices or its Birmingham headquarters.

Interfaces With Publishers: The agency actively pursues the development of electronic interfaces with publishers. Between fifteen and twenty agreements have been made for the transfer of orders on magnetic tape, encompassing some 160 publishers and approximately 10 percent of all orders originating from EBSCO. Orders on tape are dispatched on schedules specified by the publishers, usually weekly or monthly. Online links have been implemented for the transfer of claims to a number of publishers, including Elsevier, the Royal Society of Chemistry, and the New England Journal of Medicine. A number of publishers receive and respond to claims using the TELMAIL electronic mail system. EBSCO accepts publisher price information updates on magnetic tape and floppy disk. Data is currently received in these formats from Elsevier and Pergamon. Several publishers also provide journal dispatch information in machine-readable form on floppy diskette or tape. This data is loaded into EBSCO's database once a month.

THE FAXON COMPANY

Faxon offers a range of automated support services for serials acquisitions and management, including:

- management reports generated from the agency's internal automated system,

- DataLinx, which supports online access to agency files, and the online submission of orders and claims,
- SC-10 Check-in, a mainframe-based serials check-in service with automatic claiming and a journal routing capability,
- a mainframe based serials Union List service,
- MicroLinx Check-in, a standalone PC-based serials check-in, routing, and claiming system for serials management at local sites,
- INFOSERV, a database for collection development and ordering which includes the Alfred Jaeger back issues inventory,
- interfaces for data access and transfer between Faxon and other systems. Interface products and services include: EASI (Enhanced Asynchronous Software Interface) software designed to support DataLinx access and file transfer; FI$CAL, PC software for the export of data from the Faxon invoice file to spreadsheet and database management programs; and SMARTS (Serials Management and Resource Tracking System), a PC-based software package that supports the manipulation and transfer of machine-readable renewal lists.

The company has also developed electronic interfaces to support the exchange of information, orders, and claims with publishers.

Faxon indicates that its principal objective in offering these products and services is to support the company's primary business. It has found that there is a greater consolidation of services (growth in the size of accounts) and a higher retention rate among libraries that use its automation products than among the customer base as a whole. While only 10 percent of customers use Faxon's automation products and services, nearly one-third of all orders are submitted electronically. These accounts generate approximately half of Faxon's total domestic revenues. The company reports that use of its automation services has reduced redundant data entry, thus lowering order fulfillment costs.

Management Reports: Faxon's internal automated system supports a wide variety of report generation capabilities.

DataLinx: DataLinx provides online access to bibliographic and financial files mounted on Faxon's mainframe computer system. The service supports four functions:

- access to title and publisher files,
- online submission of orders, renewals, and claims,

- confidential access to individual library order and account information, and
- the LINX Courier electronic mail system.

Faxon maintains records for some 190,000 active and ceased titles. In reflection of the system's primary focus—support of subscription placement and maintenance—the files contain multiple entries for different editions and pricing packages for individual titles: separate entries for member rates and non-member rates, regular and air mail delivery, title and indexes, etc.

DataLinx supports access to *bibliographic and publisher information* in a number of formats, including:

- ALPHA TITLE—alphabetic and ISSN access,
- TKEY (Title Keyword)—keyword retrieval of all titles containing significant word(s) specified by the operator,
- TSUM (Title Summary)—complete title information including publisher, current price, ordering restrictions, and claiming information,
- MARC S—serials cataloging records in MARC format, and
- TTLR (Title Rates)—complete title pricing and history.

Publisher information may be accessed through:

- PUB (Publisher)—addresses and phone numbers for ordering and claiming, and
- TWIP (Titles Within Publisher)—retrieves all the titles offered by a particular publisher. May be searched with incomplete publisher information.

The system also provides access to bibliographic current awareness files, including:

- INFOSERV—information and abstracts for new serial publications.

Each bibliographic record contains a unique title number; publishers are identified by publisher number. Libraries can submit new *orders* and transfer and *renewal subscriptions* by keying the appropriate title number on the formatted screens supported by the LINX Courier electronic mail service. The INFOSERV file contains its own ordering module, allowing an operator to request sample issues or place an order using a single keystroke.

DataLinx also provides secure access to a number of User/ Financial files containing information about *individual subscriber accounts.* Each client's files are protected from access by other users. Available files include:

- CUST (Customer)—displays a library's ordering requirements and selection of invoicing options,
- INV (Invoice)—displays an online summary of a library's invoices,
- SCAN—displays up to three years of payment history for a particular title,
- HIST—(History) displays the master payment record, including all changes, for each subscription on file,
- HSUM (History Summary)—displays summary information from the master history record,
- SCIT (Shared Data Holdings Information)—lists titles in the centralized SC-10 check-in system as well as the clients who receive them. It provides shared holdings information for the SC-10 clients who have agreed to make this information available to other libraries,
- SC-10 Access—DataLinx clients have view-only access to the check-in screens of SC-10 users who grant permission for their records to be accessed by other libraries. This file is of assistance in determining whether to submit a claim for an item that has not yet been received, allowing an operator to check whether other libraries have recorded receipt of the issue.

The DataLinx *electronic mail* facility, LINX Courier, supports electronic communication with Faxon and also allows a library to communicate with other DataLinx users. In addition to formatted screens for the placement of new, transfer, and renewal subscriptions and claims, LINX Courier provides a free-form memo option. The system is menu-driven. Courier also supports a formatted screen for interlibrary loan applications.

DataLinx can be accessed from any personal computer or terminal with telecommunications capabilities. Both dial-up and dedicated access are supported. The service is priced at $100 per month, plus telecommunications charges. The price is reduced to $900 a year when DataLinx is purchased in conjunction with the MicroLinx standalone serials check-in system. DataLinx is provided free of charge to libraries which use the mainframe-based serials check-in service, SC-10, or the associated Linx Route service. Training is available for an additional fee.

SC-10: SC-10 is an online serials check-in system mounted on the Faxon mainframe. It supports check-in from remote sites, claim identification, and display access to the check-in records of consenting users. This last feature enables libraries to confirm the need for a claim—to check whether an issue not received by one library has been received by another SC-10 user. SC-10 also supports *union catalog applications*. A separate module, Route, offers routing functions.

SC-10 can be used to *check-in* all serials in a library's collection—those ordered through Faxon and those obtained from other sources. SC-10 is available only to libraries that use Faxon's subscription services. It handles both single and multiple copy subscriptions and can accommodate a collection of any size.

The SC-10 record format includes the following data elements:

- title and customer number,
- copy number,
- title—library form of title if different from agency form of title, or else agency form of title,
- frequency—system supplied,
- number of issues per year,
- description—a library-supplied code signifying form of receipt of material: membership, newspaper, microfiche, etc.
- call number—library-supplied, up to 30 characters in length,
- matrix—type of check-in screen display used for the title. Accords with the frequency recorded for the title.
- arrival—system-supplied indication of the number of days between receipt of one issue and the next issue. Can be changed for titles from sources other than Faxon.
- current issues—temporary location of material within the library.
- publication status,
- effective date of publication status,
- shelving location,
- binding,
- title page and index information,
- basic routing information,
- marking information for labels etc.,
- ISSN,
- Library of Congress classification—the first three characters of the LC classification number for the title are system supplied.
- alternate access points—up to 13 characters of data to describe alternative online access points such as initialisms or acronyms.
- information service lines—library-specific information used for selecting and ordering the records in printed reports. Used for details such as addresses, financial codes, subject codes, etc.

- source of material—Faxon, another agency, direct from publisher, exchange, etc.
- index and abstracts—system-supplied codes indicating indexing and abstracting service coverage.
- local library identification number(s),
- holdings—accommodates up to 148 characters of library-input holdings description.
- missing issue data, and
- comments.

A separate binding screen stores binding processing information from which a variety of binding reports can be generated.

Records may be retrieved by library form of entry, Faxon form of entry, ISSN, an alternate access term, library-assigned ID number, call number, and title number. Individual volumes of monographic series can be accessed by title, author, or call number if that data is input during check-in. Keyword searching is supported on library form of title. Records may also be retrieved using a barcode reader to scan the barcode identification printed on the covers of some journals.

SC-10 check-in records for titles listed in the Faxon title files are set up by keying the title number assigned to the item in the DataLinx title file. If a record is required for an item that does not appear in this file, the relevant check-in record is created by Faxon staff.

Once the appropriate record is retrieved, check-in is accomplished by an operator keying the last two digits of the current year, the numbers of the appropriate column and line on the check-in display, and the date and/volume or number of the issue. When data entry is completed, the screen displays an updated check-in record. The date on which an issue is checked in is added automatically.

The system accommodates check-in of monographs in series and dailies using similar procedures. The format for monographs in series permits the input of details such as author, title, ISBN, and item call number. If entered during check-in, these elements can be used to retrieve the records at a later date. The system handles other special check-in situations including the receipt of indexes and supplements, and the management of membership subscriptions.

During check-in, SC-10 displays the appropriate local processing information such as call numbers and routing information, labelling information, etc. for the operator to follow. If required, labels and routing slips can be printed from the terminal.

SC-10 uses an algorithm based on the date of last check-in and frequency and arrival data to identify overdue materials that need to be claimed. It also allows for an operator who recognizes gaps in receipts to flag such gaps for *claiming*.

A weekly Claims Warning System Gap report lists all of a library's SC-10 titles that have been flagged by an operator, and a biweekly Claims Warning System Lapses report lists titles for which expected issues have not been recorded within the time parameters established by SC-10. The lapse report covers both active subscriptions and new subscriptions that were scheduled to become operational during the period covered by the report. SC-10 also generates a semiannual list of Irregulars to be Reviewed showing titles with an irregular frequency against which there has been no check-in activity for the previous six months.

Claiming action depends on the source of the title. Faxon handles claim preparation, dispatch, and reporting for titles acquired through Faxon; a library must prepare its own claims for items from other sources. DataLinx publisher files can be accessed to determine the appropriate claiming address for claims prepared by a library. If a library wishes to use SC-10 claim tracking facilities to monitor library-generated claims, it must also record details of its claims in the system. SC-10 claim monitoring capabilities include biweekly reports of all first, second, and third claims that have been outstanding for 56 days or more. An activity report, issued semimonthly, summarizes the specific claim action Faxon has initiated during the previous two-week period.

SC-10 generates a variety of other management and statistical reports to aid users in serials control. Available reports include a master list of titles and monthly check-in statistics.

Rudimentary *routing* data can be accommodated in the basic SC-10 record. A separate Linx Route module supports more sophisticated routing functions with prioritization and global change capabilities. This separately priced service allows SC-10 users to print routing slips as issues are checked in. Route supports automatic prioritization of readers by rank or location. A variety of reports provide workflow and routing data.

Libraries can access SC-10 from a dedicated terminal or a personal computer connected to the mainframe using dedicated leased lines, a network connection, or dial access. Virtually all SC-10 customers use leased lines. Faxon recommends that users assign one terminal or personal computer for each 5,000 titles controlled on SC-10.

SC-10 usage is billed on a per-record basis, plus telecommunications charges. Prices start at $.30 per record per month for up to

1,000 active records. A lower per-record price can be negotiated for large accounts. Additional charges apply to Route. A leased line costs approximately $350 per month. Training is available. Training costs vary depending on the size and composition of the group trained. Pricing for Route uses the same fee structure as SC-10, $.30 per Route record per month.

Serials Union List: Individual libraries that use SC-10 for serials check-in and give permission for other users to search their files are effectively participants in an online union list of serials. Interlibrary loan request transmission among such libraries is facilitated by the availability of a formatted interlibrary loan request screen on the LINX Courier electronic mail system.

Faxon also offers a mainframe-based system specifically designed as an online union list. Union list records can be accessed by title number (a required element in all union list records), ISSN, Library of Congress card number, union list control number, and title. The system accommodates the following local information elements: location and sublocation codes, call number, acquisitions status indicator, summary holdings statement, cumulative holdings, and copy-specific comments.

Faxon requires that one library in a union list group assumes editorial responsibility for the file. This entails monitoring member input to see that it conforms to group standards and policies and to ensure that each new title is input with the appropriate title number. To assist the editorial site, Faxon provides online access to its resource file of MARC records and the title file at no charge other than telecommunications costs. If a library reports a title that is not in the title file, Faxon will add the title to that file and assign it an appropriate number.

A variety of union list outputs is available including fiche, hardcopy, or magnetic tape. Current output formats include union lists, keyword indexes, individual library listings, and statistical and management reports.

Union list online charges vary with the number of records on the system. Discounts apply for volume use. The maximum monthly charge for a library's union list records is $.05 per active record and $.025 for inactive records. Dial access is available via WATS for $20 per hour. Dedicated lines may be leased for $350 a month. Offline products are charged at $.018 per unique title, holding, cross reference, and keyword for processing. Charges also apply for the output media and handling.

MicroLinx: MicroLinx is a standalone PC-based serial control system suitable for libraries with 5,000 or fewer current serials. The system is prediction-based, allowing *check-in* of an issue to be recorded with a single keystroke. It handles both single and multiple copy subscriptions, and recognizes and flags missing issues for claiming. In addition to check-in and claiming, MicroLinx also supports routing, binding, fiscal control, and the generation of management reports. MicroLinx is available only to libraries that use Faxon's subscription services.

MicroLinx accommodates detailed, MARC-compatible information about each title. A wide variety of bibliographic fields is provided, including a notes field for storing any descriptive data chosen by a library. In addition to standard identifiers such as ISSN, LCCN, and call number, a library may enter up to three local identification numbers for each title. The system allows selection from over twenty search criteria including keywords, record number, ISSN, subject, and language for locating titles or copies. Records can also be retrieved by scanning the machine-readable barcodes printed on the covers of many journals. The system predicts issue enumeration; once the appropriate check-in screen is retrieved, check-in can be completed with a single keystroke.

Records may be created by operator keying, or Faxon can supply machine-readable records from a variety of sources. Detailed financial data can also be recorded; MicroLinx accommodates invoice data, including currency, exchange rate, and service charges. Separate invoice data can be maintained for each copy, complete with the relevant subscription start and end dates, fund numbers, and other pertinent data. For titles ordered from Faxon, invoice information is loaded into MicroLinx prior to its shipment to the library. This data may be updated by loading a machine-readable version of the library's annual renewal invoice—available on diskette or by electronic transfer.

MicroLinx uses prediction algorithms to recognize past-due issues and flags these for potential *claiming*. A library may generate claim letters for dispatch direct to publishers. Claims for titles ordered through Faxon can be forwarded to Faxon on diskette or through an electronic linkage between MicroLinx and the agency's mainframe system.

Call number labels can be printed during check-in or as a batch at the end of a check-in session. The system also produces binding slips and binding status reports. Binding slips provide detailed specifications, including a facsimile spine imprint.

The standard MicroLinx system offers basic *routing* capabilities including the printing of routing slips. A full-function, separately priced Route module provides greater flexibility and more sophisticated features linking reader, title/copy and subject lists in various relationships. The module supports multi-copy route slip maintenance, route slip and label printing, automatic assignment of readers to copies, prioritization of readers on slips, and subject assignment of readers to titles. Standard report formats allow sorting of routing data by department, fund, title, subject, or reader. Routing statistics may also be generated.

MicroLinx produces a variety of reports including title listings, maintenance reports, file statistics, and renewal information. More than twenty different reports have been defined, each with several sorting and selection options.

While designed to operate as a standalone system, MicroLinx also supports online access to the DataLinx service for an annual fee of $900 plus telecommunications charges. Use of the Courier electronic mail service is billed at $20 per hour.

MicroLinx operates on IBM personal computers and compatible machines with 286 or 386 processors. The basic software package is priced at $1,895, with an annual renewal fee of $800; the software with extended routing capabilities costs $2,095, with an annual renewal fee of $900. The telecommunications package to support communication between MicroLinx and Faxon requires software priced at $500 and a Hayes compatible modem. Two-day regional training sessions are required for MicroLinx users, the price varies according to group size and location.

INFOSERV: An online information system that provides access to specialized files and services. INFORSERV is provided to Faxon clients at no charge other than telecommunications charges of $20 per hour. The following databases are available on INFOSERV:

- New and Revised Title File
- Faxon Online Librarian's Guide
- Alfred Jaeger Back Issue File
- Biomedical Document Delivery Service.

The system supports keyword searching and online order submission.

Designed to support collection development and acquisitions, the New and Revised Title file contains entries for *new* serials first published in the past three years and publications which have changed their names in the same period. Entries include pricing data and abstracts, and may be accessed by keyword searches of title, publisher, or abstracts, through ISSN, or by Library of Congress subject classification code. Publishers have the opportunity to include additional screens of advertising data—tables of contents, editorial board membership, and longer abstracts, for instance—for each title. INFOSERV provides formatted screens for sample issue requests and placement of subscription orders.

The *Faxon Online Librarian's Guide* is an online version of the company's printed title catalog. To be included in the file, titles must have at least three active subscribers. The file can be searched by title, publisher and abstract keywords, ISSN, or Library of Congress classification code. INFOSERV provides formatted screens for online ordering of the titles in the Guide.

The Alfred Jaeger Back Issue file is an inventory of bound *back issues* available from Jaeger. The system allows inspection of the inventory and supports the submission of requests for quotes to Jaeger.

The *Biomedical Document Delivery Service* provides a list of journal titles for which article reprints are available from Information on Demand (IOD). Orders for titles covered by the service are entered on INFOSERV and sent to IOD for fulfillment. Twenty-four hour turnaround is guaranteed for orders entered before 2:00 p.m. Reprints are billed at $9.00 per article plus any copyright payments that apply. Users may request overnight delivery for an additional charge.

Library System Interfaces: Faxon is active in the development of interfaces to link its systems with those of libraries. Products and services focusing on this objective include:

- machine-readable invoicing data,
- machine-readable renewal listings,
- record/retrospective conversion,
- transfer of bibliographic and holdings data among Faxon systems—SC-10, MicroLinx, and the Serials Union List system—and between these systems and local library systems,
- support for PC-based file transfer between Faxon and local libraries, and
- the provision of gateways from local automated library systems to Faxon's online services.

Faxon provides *machine-readable invoicing data* for loading into local library and management systems. Unless otherwise requested, the data is distributed in a Faxon-defined format. The data includes changes in title and frequency, as well as price and fund account allocations. Output media options include magnetic tape, tape cartridges, diskettes, and online electronic transfer. Annual invoicing data is supplied free of charge; quarterly updates are billed at $200 per year, and monthly updates are available for $400 a year.

Faxon invoice data can be loaded directly into MicroLinx. A PC-based program, FI$CAL, also allows machine-readable invoices to be loaded to commercial database or spreadsheet programs for financial planning and analysis. Priced at $200, FI$CAL formats data for loading to Lotus 1-2-3, Symphony, dBase II or III, and other database and spreadsheet software that accepts ASCII files.

In addition to its generic format, Faxon offers system-specific formats to support the loading of invoice data to popular local automated library systems. Among the systems for which such capabilities are operational are Data Trek, Geac, Innovacq, NOTIS, Orion, and Philsom.

Renewal lists are also available in machine-readable format, the SMARTS (Serials Management and Resource Tracking System) PC-based software allows quote and renewal information to be downloaded from the Faxon system, edited, and uploaded to Faxon for processing. The software supports the addition and change of title and copy information. SMARTS is available for $449, including a training package.

Faxon can supply *machine-readable serials records* from its internal files and MARC records from the CONSER database. It can also convert records from the SC-10 and Route systems for export to other systems. Faxon's database creation services carry a set-up charge of $300 plus a fee of $.20 per record.

MARC serial records can be selected to match library-specified title numbers, ISSNs, or all titles for which a library uses a specific Faxon service (such as all titles ordered through Faxon or all titles that a library maintains on the SC-10 or Union List service). Records are output in LC MARC format on tape, cartridge, or floppy disk. Interfaces have been developed for the direct transfer of MARC records from the MicroLinx serials check-in system to local library systems that accept MARC formatted serials records.

Holdings data recorded in Faxon's serials control systems can be output in the MARC holdings format. Faxon-developed interfaces allow the exchange of bibliographic and holdings data among Faxon systems—MicroLinx data uploaded to the Union List service, SC-10 records prepared for loading to MicroLinx, etc.—and support the loading of bibliographic and holdings data to local automated library systems and external union lists.

Faxon's use of the MARC format for output of bibliographic and holdings data allows the transfer of records from Faxon systems to other systems that accept MARC formatted records. In addition, system-specific interfaces have been developed to load

Faxon bibliographic and holdings data to a number of automated library systems, including CLSI, Inmagic, Innovative Interfaces, SIRSI, VTLS, and Ulisys. These interfaces allow libraries to transfer bibliographic and holdings data from SC-10 or MicroLinx to their online catalogs.

EASI (Enhanced Asynchronous Software Interface) is a proprietary communications software package which standardizes file transfer and online access procedures for clients accessing Faxon services from a personal computer and a Hayes compatible modem. Primarily used in conjunction with MicroLinx, EASI may also be used with SMARTS and in other file transfer applications. A $500 license applies for the first year of EASI use; thereafter, the annual fee is $50. EASI attracts connect time charges of $20 an hour.

To facilitate access to its online services, Faxon has developed *gateways* that allow any terminal on a local library system to communicate with Faxon over dedicated telecommunications lines. In addition to providing library system wide access to DataLinx, such connections allow a local system terminal to be used for serials check-in on SC-10. Libraries with systems that support the appropriate modems and telecommunications software can also access Faxon's online services through dial access. Faxon also offers interfaces that allow a single PC workstation to serve as a MicroLinx check-in station, a terminal on a local library system, and a Faxon access terminal. The capability is operational for a number of systems including Geac and WLN.

The availability of interfaces between Faxon and other vendors and networks changes daily as development, testing, and implementation are completed. Up-to-date information on the status of specific interfaces is available from Faxon sales representatives or the company's Westwood headquarters.

Interfaces With Publishers: Faxon is active in the development of interfaces with publishers for the transfer of machine-readable bibliographic, order, claiming, and schedule data. Electronic transmission is also used in funds transfer. Although online interfaces have been developed with a number of publishers, the most common form of communication with large publishers is by magnetic tape transfer.

INDEX